Walks in the Country
HEART OF ENGLAND

Walks in the Country
HEART OF ENGLAND

Richard Shurey

COUNTRYSIDE BOOKS
NEWBURY, BERKSHIRE

First published 1998
© Richard Shurey 1998

COUNTRYSIDE BOOKS
3 Catherine Road
Newbury, Berkshire

ISBN 1 85306 531 5

Designed by Graham Whiteman
Photographs and maps by the author

Front cover photo of the river Teme, near
Worcester, taken by Bill Meadows

Produced through MRM Associates Ltd., Reading
Printed by J. W. Arrowsmith Ltd., Bristol

Contents

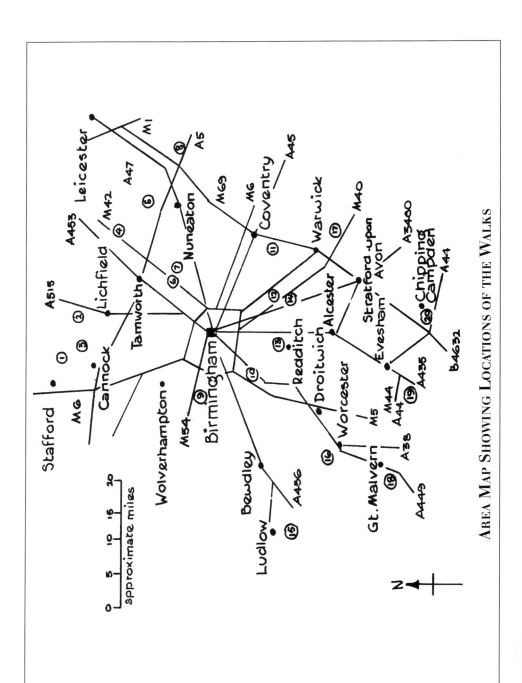

AREA MAP SHOWING LOCATIONS OF THE WALKS

Publisher's Note

We hope that you obtain considerable enjoyment from this book; great care has been taken in its preparation. Although at the time of publication all routes followed public rights of way or permited paths, diversion orders can be made and permissions withdrawn.

We cannot of course be held responsible for such diversion orders and any inaccuracies in the text which result from these or any other changes to the routes nor any damage which might result from walkers trespassing on private property. We are anxious though that all details covering the walks are kept up to date and would therefore welcome information from readers which would be relevant to future editions.

Introduction

The Heart of England may be as far from the sea as you can get in the Kingdom – so coastal scenery is not available – but how fortunate we are to have so many other terrains to add variety, to these 20 circular walks.

Some of the rambles are along the towing paths of the ancient canals. Constructed two centuries ago, they now provide wonderful escape routes from the bustling fast lane of today's life. There are more views of soothing water when the walk borders reservoirs or quarry pools on which yachts skim when a breeze is caught.

A particularly interesting excursion is to the historic battle site at Bosworth, where Richard III was killed – the last monarch of England to die when leading his troops into battle. Nearby it is possible to have the thrill of a journey on a train hauled by a steam locomotive.

There are strolls along highways like the Fosse Way and Ryknild Street which echoed to the sounds of marching Roman legionaries. Later the invaders were the Normans and we can explore the countryside around two of their finest castles at Kenilworth and Ludlow.

This lovely countryside gave inspiration to many of our greatest writers and composers. Warwickshire is justly proud to have had William Shakespeare as one of its sons. A.E. Housman told of 'summertime on Bredon' and Elgar spent many hours exploring the byways around his home and high on the Malvern ridge. There are walks here which follow in their footsteps.

There is also the wild grandeur of Cannock Chase and rambles to great gardens and houses like Packwood, Shugborough and Baddesley Clinton and to the sites of former places of splendour and glory where the great house or castle has perished long ago.

Most of the rambles go through little villages; these again reflect the splendid variety of the Heart of England. We find delightful cottages of Cotswold stone and thatch where roses climb to the eaves; there are black and white timber-framed houses so synonymous with Worcestershire and elegant Georgian buildings. The English pub thrives in the villages even if the modernised and re-named town hostelries have lost their charm!

The relevant OS Landranger map is recommended for each walk, to accompany the sketch maps provided. Special sections mention places to find food and drink on the route, or places of interest nearby.

So enough chat – everyone (especially the dog!) is raring to start to explore the lovely countryside of the Heart of England. Select a walk, pull on the boots and off we go – but don't forget the waterproofs, it has been known to rain here just now and again. Happy rambling!

Richard Shurey

Walk 1
STAFFORDSHIRE'S FORESTS AND WATERWAYS
Length : 4 or 9 miles

Shugborough Hall.

GETTING THERE: Milford is 3½ miles east along the A513 from Stafford.

PARKING: There is a car park along the lane to the south of the main road in the village.

MAPS: OS Landranger – Stafford and Telford 127 and Derby and Burton upon Trent area 128 (GR 973210).

he Staffordshire and Worcester-shire Canal (which runs alongside the meanders of the river Sow) and the Trent and Mersey Canal were both engineered by James Brindley towards the end of the 18th century, although he never lived to see the completion of the latter. This was considered to be his masterpiece,

being a cross-country waterway. The Staffordshire and Worcestershire Canal (a contour canal and therefore sinuous) was rather unusual in that it was highly profitable, perhaps because it was linked to so many other canals in the Midands, and paid good dividends to the shareholders for many years.

FOOD and DRINK

There are inns at Milford, Great Haywood and Little Haywood. The Fox and Hounds at Great Haywood is conveniently placed on the route. The 'specials' board by the bar is worth looking at. Here, vegetarians are well catered for – the vegetable tagliatelle with mushroom and cream sauce sounds tempting! Telephone: 01889 881252. There is a cafe at Milford and an ice cream van can often be spotted in the car park. Refreshments are obtainable at Shugborough Hall and Farm and there are also picnic sites in the park.

This walk follows the canal tow paths, where the going is easy with much of interest; in summertime the waterways are popular with tourists who seek an escape along tranquil ways from the noisy roads. In the cooler months of the year nature reigns and numerous species of waterfowl will be seen.

A visit can be made to the delightful parkland of Shugborough and the great Hall, now National Trust property (see Places of Interest). There

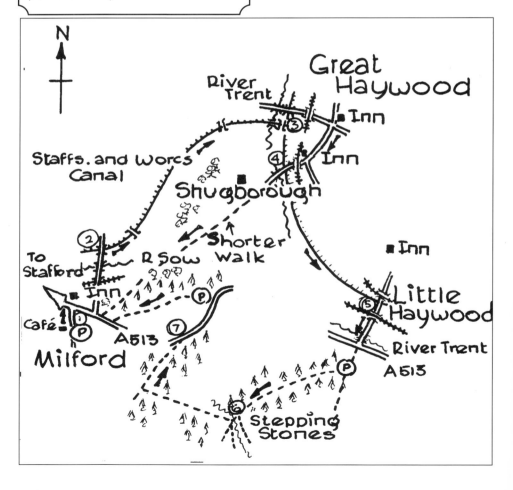

are 900 acres of typical English park-land wth fine gardens, shrubs and trees.

The later section of the walk, bring-ing you back to Milford, is through the deep forests and over the wild grandeur of the bleak moorland of Cannock Chase. This was once a royal forest which is rather surprising as usually the term 'chase' was reserved for woodland owned by a commoner. Edward I decreed that all the wolves on the Chase should be hunted down and destroyed to protect the deer. We can still see the herds of deer today; they would be descendants of the ani-mals introduced into this countryside by the Romans and later hunted by royalty.

In 1958 it was officially designated as an Area of Outstanding Natural Beauty. The soil is very gravelly and was considered too poor for agricul-ture, but the acid soils support vast tracts of heather which are very beau-tiful when in full bloom.

THE WALK

1 From the car park walk a few steps eastwards along the A513. Turn left along a lane. Go over the railway and the river Sow. Just before the canal bridge go down steps left to the towing path.

2 Turn right to go under the road. Follow the towing path of the Stafford-shire and Worcestershire Canal for about 2 miles. The path goes over the river to a junction of canals.

3 Go left over a bridge to cross the 'old' canal and join the 'new' canal, the

Trent and Mersey. Walk along the towing path to the road. Turn right to the village of Great Haywood. At a junction of roads turn right. By an inn turn right again.

4 Keep ahead to pass under the rail-way to the canal. Decision time! For the shorter walk stay on in the same direction to pass over the old pack-horse bridge. This is the 17th century Essex Bridge, named after the Earl of Essex who built it. Although only 14 of the original 40 arches remain it is said to be the longest surviving packhorse bridge in the land. This way leads to Shugborough Hall and the park, where a vehicle way takes you back to the main road and Milford.

PLACES of INTEREST

Shugborough Hall is a charming house set in the 900-acre park and was built on the site of the Bishop of Lichfield's palace in 1748. It was greatly enlarged in 1750 and altered to the Regency style after 1790 by Samuel Wyatt for the first Viscount Anson. Although owned by the National Trust it is financed and administered by Staffordshire County Council. It is open daily from end March until end September 11 am to 5pm, and on Sundays only in October. Telephone: 01889 881388. In **Shugborough Park** is the Georgian farmstead which was built in 1805 for Thomas, Viscount Anson. It is now a wonderful Working Farm Museum. Here you can see a working corn mill and (at close hand) domestic and rare breeds of cattle and poultry. **Milford** is the starting place of a popular long distance pathway. The Heart of England Way winds an attractive route through Middle England to end 100 miles later at Bourton-on-the-Water in Gloucestershire.

The neo-Grecian monument designed by James Stuart that stands in the grounds of Shugborough Park.

For the longer walk gain the towing path and follow beside the waterway to the next road bridge at Little Haywood.

5 Leave the canal. The lane goes under the railway and over the river Trent to the A513. Cross to the vehicle way to the car park. Continue to the far right-hand corner and go past the barrier. Follow the bold track to the brook at Stepping Stones.

6 There is a meeting of tracks. Turn right (signed as the Staffordshire Way). At another junction of tracks bear right (still Staffordshire Way) to a car park and the A513.

7 Turn right. After 300 yards turn left along a wide track to a car park (Cold Man's Slade). Keep ahead past a barrier and walk along a bold track. The track borders Shugborough Park to the road. Turn right back to Milford.

Walk 2
ABBOTS BROMLEY AND BLITHFIELD
Length : 8½ or 5½ miles

Blithfield Reservoir.

GETTING THERE: Abbots Bromley is 6 miles north of Rugeley along the B5014.

PARKING: Streetside in Abbots Bromley. The walk starts by the Butter Cross.

MAP: OS Landranger – Derby and Burton upon Trent area 128 (GR 080245).

Abbots Bromley is a fascinating place where it is said 'little changes'. Certainly here the heritage of our land is maintained although I never heard the curfew bell which the records say is tolled each evening!

The church of St Nicholas overlooks the town. It is on a Saxon site and there are Norman stones still to be seen, but much of today's church dates from the diligent Victorian restoration of the last century. Nearby is the Butter Cross marking the old market place. There is a wealth of beautiful buildings in the town, many of them listed. Perhaps the real gem is the timber-framed Goats Head Inn.

The walk goes from Abbots Bromley through the valley of the river Blithe. In 1953 a huge dam was constructed across the vale and Staffordshire's largest sheet of water was the result. Part of the parkland of Blithfield was inundated leaving the fine Hall rather isolated, but the resulting reservoir now gives much of the county its water supply – it covers 800 acres and stores 4,000 million gallons of water.

There are good views of the reservoir on the walk and the northern shores are particularly attractive where the wooded hills dip down to the water. Blithfield gives sport for the fishermen and yachts are sailed and raced. In addition (like so many reservoirs) Blithfield is the home of many species of wildfowl. Because of this it is a Site of Special Scientific Interest.

The walk then passes through the area of water meadows bordering the meanders of the river Blithe after it tumbles from the reservoir. With little disturbance this is a rich place for wildlife. Rabbits abound and there are badger sets in the banks. Birdlife too finds a ready habitat here and the elu-sive kingfisher may be spotted along the river banks. Herons are quite common rising slowly into the sky.

The walk southwards is along the route of the Staffordshire Way, where the paths are well maintained and waymarked, and the return route is mainly along narrow country lanes.

THE WALK

1 The walk starts from the Butter Cross. Continue to the church and go through the lych gate to the church-yard. Swing left along the path to go in front of the church. Crossing the churchyard diagonally, go through a kissing gate.

2 Stay on the path, then go over a stile on the left after about 60 yards. Cross a field then use the bridge to cross a brook, then go over a stile. On a lane turn right.

3 By a cattle grid climb a stile on the left. Walk along a track to a road. Turn right for about 100 yards then go left over a stile. Follow the arrowed way over two fields, then climb a stile. Keep

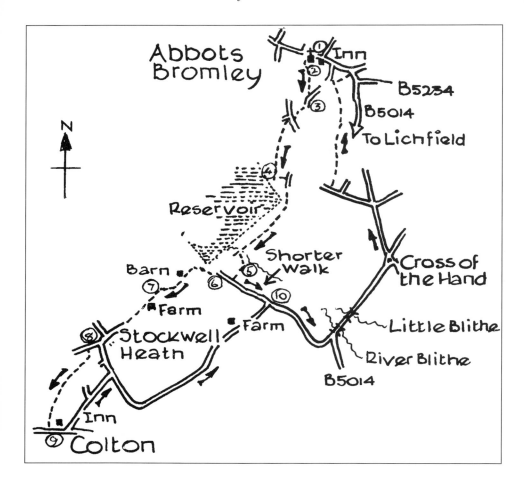

on in the same direction alongside a left-hand hedge to a green road. At the end climb a stile to a lane.

4 Turn left, then right along a road. When a hedge ends on the left go left, then at once right. Go over a stile, then continue left along a bold wide track. Follow the track over the river bridge. At once turn left to follow the river-bank downstream.

5 After about 200 yards swing right over the open field to go over a stile. Walk alongside a left-hand hedge to a road. For the shorter walk turn left to point 10 below. For the longer walk turn right along the road. Within 400 yards climb a stile left, then continue right by a fence.

6 When the fence goes right maintain the old direction, then follow the way-mark direction to walk up the incline. This is a good viewpoint for the reser-voir. Climb a stile by a barn and walk

The Butter Cross, Abbots Bromley.

alongside a right-hand fence to a corner stile. Walk alongside a hedge then go over a bridge.

7 Walk at the side of a left-hand ditch. Walk through another field (still by the ditch) and climb a stile to a lane. Keep ahead along the lane. At a junction turn left to Stockwell Heath.

8 Go past the pond then right along Moor Lane. Within a few steps the next path is left through a gate. Continue to a stream and go over the bridge. Veer right to climb a stile then go through a field to another stile. Follow the path waymarked through several fields to a road at Colton.

9 Turn left to pass an inn, then go left at a junction. Look for a signed path on the right to a lane. Turn right. Follow the lane to a junction to join the shorter route.

10 Turn right to the B5014. Turn left. Cross the river to the junction of Cross of the Hand. Keep on the B5014. Within ½ mile take a lane left. Just past a junction take a signed path right. Over a stile take the arrowed direction across fields. Nearing Abbots Bromley walk alongside a left-hand hedge to emerge on a vehicle track over a stile to the left of a house. Follow the vehicle way back to Abbots Bromley.

Walk 3
THE TOP OF CANNOCK CHASE
Length : 5 miles

A happy trio at the start of the walk.

GETTING THERE: Midway between Rugeley and Lichfield on the A51 take a lane signed to Cannock Wood. At Cannock Wood follow the signs to Castle Ring.

PARKING: There is a car park at Castle Ring.

MAP: OS Landranger – Derby and Burton upon Trent area 128 (GR 045126)

The Iron Age fort which crowns the 800 foot high hill at Castle Ring is surrounded by vast pine woods. No doubt when the earthworks were constructed about 2,000 years ago the views were uninterrupted far over the Vale of Trent, which made this such an important strategic site. It is high too – this is the loftiest point of Cannock Chase.

Much of the Chase has been left as wild countryside but there is a contrast with the woods planted (many between the wars) by the Forestry Commission. Most of this walk is through the plantations of pine woods

FOOD and DRINK

The Park Gate Inn, near the start of the walk, stands at a height of 800 ft above sea level and gives a wonderful view down the valley. The building dates from 1640 and has an interesting history, once being part of the estate of the Marquis of Anglesey. The decor of modern. Being far from the sea, it is a little surprising that the place has such a fine reputation for its fish dishes, with the Big Catch Platter being very popular. Telephone: 01543 682223.

– so sweet-smelling especially after rain. There are brooks which tumble down from the high land over gravelly beds and pools which attract wildfowl.

The acid soils of Cannock Chase were always considered too poor for agriculture but there was a distinctive type of sheep which fed on the meagre grass in great numbers. Cannock was a thriving market town for their sale. There were also once great coal mining and ironworking industries here.

With arable farming difficult there was no pressure to enclose the open land, which gives that splendid sense of isolation on the Chase. Here there are bracken slopes and heather thrives away from the pine plantations. There are pockets of deciduous trees but in the main it is the different varieties of pines (such as the Scots and Corsican pines) which from above give a delightful vista of many shades of green.

From Castle Ring the walk takes you down to explore this lovely wooded area. The route also goes along the wide track called Marquis Drive, a long carriage way created by the Marquis of Anglesey on his estate of Beaudesert, before returning through forestland to the ancient hill fort.

THE WALK

1 Take time to explore this hill-fort. Then, keeping the fortification on your right, walk along the broad path which is signed as being on the route of the Heart of England Way.

2 Cross another wide path and enter the forestlands. Deer still roam here. They are elusive animals and with their keen sense of hearing and smell tend to keep away from the more popular areas although many are killed on the roads each year by motor vehicles. They mate in the late autumn when many fights can develop over territorial rights. Early morning is the best time to see a herd of the fallow deer. Keep ahead to rejoin the forest 'road'. Maintain the heading along this track which goes through plantations of Scots and Corsican pines.

3 The 'road' drops sharply downhill and crosses brooks. Climb out of the valley and continue to a road. Do not join the road but take the path (still Heart of England Way) to the right. At a junction turn left along the track to a road. Go right to a crossroads.

4 Turn left along a bold, wide vehicle track. This is Marquis Drive. Within ½ mile you pass a house. At a junction of tracks take the left-hand fork. Pass a mere and keep on the main track and alongside a brook.

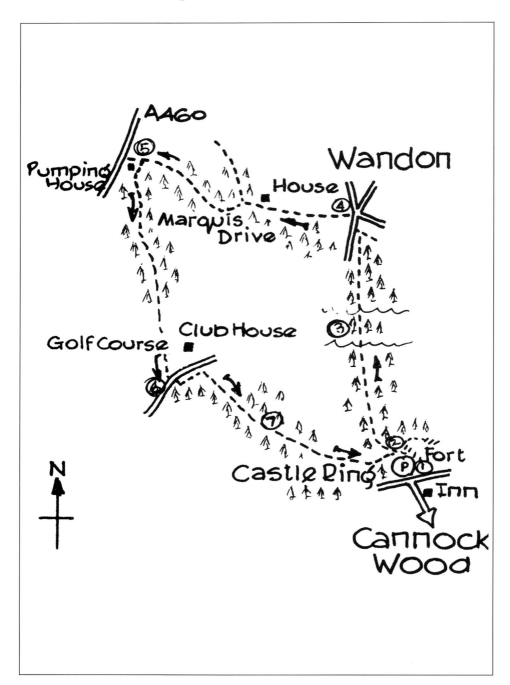

5 Just before a main road take a wide track left through a barrier. Climb the rise and then swing right with a pumping station on the right-hand side. By a house is a junction of ways. Walk along the track over the crest of the hill. Keep ahead to go by a golf course to a road.

6 Turn left. Opposite the golf club drive join a track on the right which runs alongside the road. Within 400 yards (by a barrier) turn sharp right along a bold track, now walking away from the road.

7 Maintain the heading when crossing other tracks. Now, climbing, join the outward route and retrace your steps to Castle Ring and the car park.

Walk 4
WE'RE ALL GOING TO THE ZOO
Length : 5½ miles

Austrey.

GETTING THERE: From Junction 11 of the M42 go south-eastwards along the A444. Within 2½ miles take a lane to the left signed to Norton-Juxta-Twycross where the walk starts.

PARKING: Along the quiet roadsides in Norton-Juxta-Twycross village.

MAP: OS Landranger – Leicester and Coventry area 140 (GR 323070).

The peaceful countryside here on the borders of Leicestershire and Warwickshire is a mainly open arable landscape, although there are still the white-faced Leicestershire breed of sheep and Friesian cattle to be seen in the fields.

The walk starts in the attractive village of Norton-Juxta-Twycross. Its rather lengthy name merely signifies that it is a place north of the village of Twycross. Norton has many attractive houses – I liked the grandeur of several especially the dollshouse-look of Bay Tree House near the pub. The church has a wonderful light interior with large clear windows, but especially attractive is the large stained glass window above the altar.

The route takes you past Twycross Zoo (see Places of Interest) and out into the countryside to another picturesque village. Austrey has timber-framed cottages and Georgian terraces, with an especially attractive corner by the thatch-roofed inn in the centre of the village. The church, dedicated to St Nicholas, has a graceful broach spire above an Early English tower and dominates the village. The building has a 14th century nave and glass in the windows and the font date from the same era. In front of the inn at Austrey is the village cross which has stood there since the 15th century.

The return route is via Appleby Hill, where there is a huge radio aerial. It carries radio, television and telecommunication signals, and resembles a rocket about to be launched.

THE WALK

1 From the inn cross the road to a signed footpath. Walk along a hedged and fenced way (Bay Tree House is to the right). The path becomes a vehicle way to Main Street. Almost opposite, go down Chapel Lane.

2 At the end take a footpath at the left of a white house. Walk alongside a fence to a stile into a pasture. Walk the length. Go over a wire fence then climb a stile in the far left-hand corner to a road.

3 Turn right to Twycross Zoo. Turn left at the crossroads signed to Orton. Within ½ mile pass a farm on the right. A few steps past a footpath sign go through a metal gate on the right.

4 In a pasture turn left; within 100 yards turn right through a hedge gap. Cross the field to a stile. Maintain the heading alongside a hedge to a stile and waymark post. Carefully take the arrowed direction across a large arable

PLACES of INTEREST

Twycross Zoo is open every day of the year. This is not the usual type of zoo for here it is said that 'the animals are ambassadors for conservation in the wild'. There are special programmes to breed species that are threatened with extinction, and also a welcome for young people to come on an educational programme with teaching sessions and 'hands on' activities involving animals. Telephone: 01827 880250. The grouping of animals ensures that there is not a lot of walking to see all the many attractions. Children especially enjoy the feeding sessions of the sea-lions, seals and penguins and there is an adventure playground for youngsters under eleven.

The east window of the church in Norton-Juxta-Twycross.

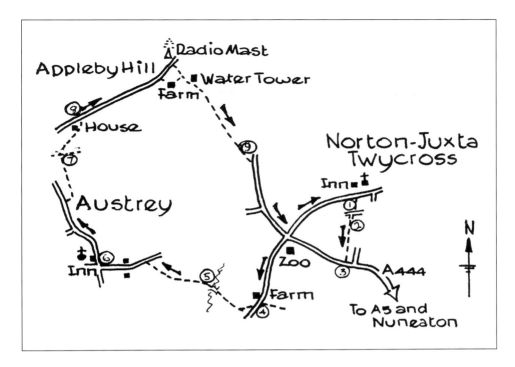

field to a bridge over a ditch.

5 Follow a way near the right-hand hedge and field-border bank then veer right (aiming to the right of a distant church spire) to reach a lane. Turn left and drop down to Austrey.

6 Turn right at a junction and keep to the right of the inn. Within 300 yards and by a house called 'Farthings', a footpath starts on the right. The path goes left at the rear of houses to a farm road. Cross to the opposite stile.

7 In the field bear right aiming to the right of houses to reach a lane.

8 Turn right and climb Appleby Hill. Just past the drive of Hill Farm a bridleway is signed down a cart track. (The tall 'rocket' aerial is nearby.) Pass by a water tower and follow right-hand hedges.

9 Descend to a road. Turn right. Take care as this is a busy highway. At a crossroads turn left along a lane to return to Norton-Juxta-Twycross.

Walk 5
RELIVE THE BATTLE OF BOSWORTH
Length : 8 miles

The Battle of Bosworth site.

GETTING THERE: From the M69 (Junction 1) and Hinkley go northwards along the A447. Turn left along the B585 to Market Bosworth.

PARKING: There is a car park at Market Bosworth Park.

MAP: OS Landranger – Leicester and Coventry 140 (GR 407031).

There are gentle uplands in the countryside around the site of the Battle of Bosworth, which was the decisive encounter in 1485 in the Wars of the Roses. The higher land was an important factor. Richard III marched his men to Sutton Cheney then occupied the nearby Ambion Hill early on the morning of 22nd August 1485. His fickle ally Lord Stanley stood off on a nearby ridge waiting to see which way the fight was going. Henry Tudor persuaded Stanley to change sides and the rest, as they say, is history. Today the site has a unique and exciting living battle trail (see Places of Interest).

The starting place of Market Bosworth is renowned for its attractive floral displays in the Leicestershire in Bloom Competition. There is an old grammar school, founded in early Tudor times and which was funded by Sir Wolstan Dixie in 1601. For a few months Samuel Johnson was a teacher here (but resigned it is said through boredom!). There is an ancient market cross and the spire of the 15th century church overlooks the town.

Also on this walk you can enjoy the delights of the Battlefield Line. The steam and diesel trains run along a 4 mile track near Bosworth Field – you can even cheat a little to shorten the walk!

The route goes along the towing path of the Ashby de la Zouch Canal before returning to Market Bosworth. This 50-mile long waterway was constructed under an Act of Parliament in 1794 and runs through pleasant farmland. Being a contour canal, it has very few locks. It is always full of interest, especially in the summer months as this is a popular holiday route. The waterway also attracts many species of wildlife.

THE WALK

1 From the Market Square walk southwards away from the old grammar school. There is a junction of roads; keep ahead along a lane signed as a gated road. There is soon a gate to pass through but do ensure it is closed again as cattle roam beside the lane.

2 Within ¾ mile look for a footpath over a railed footbridge on the right. In the field turn left to walk alongside the hedge. Over a superfluous stile keep ahead in the next field. At a corner turn right. After 50 yards go through a hedge gap to regain the old direction. Go over a rather wobbly plank bridge and maintain the heading over an open field to the corner of a hedge which juts into our field.

3 Follow waymarks (yellow arrows and yellow-topped posts) through further fields. There is an open field then a stile to a lane. Cross to the

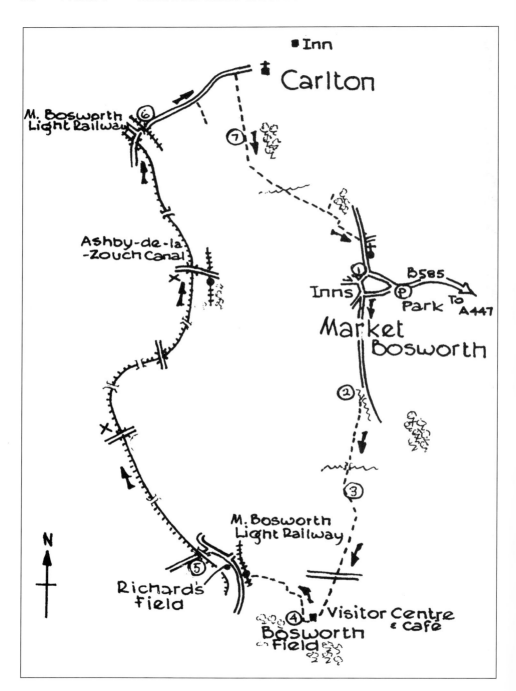

The memorial stone in Richard's Field.

vehicle way opposite which leads to the Visitor Centre (in a former farmhouse) of the Battlefield site. Go to the right of the Visitor Centre and through a car park. In the bottom right-hand corner pick up a cinder path going right.

4 Follow the path past the strategic battle points to descend to the railway at Shenton station. (You can catch a train back to Market Bosworth station if you are short of time.) Pass through gates to cross the tracks and proceed to the lane. Turn right to go by Richard's Field. Keep ahead on the lane. At the second junction turn left (signed Shenton) to pass under a bridge.

5 At once turn left to climb steps to the towing path of the canal. Turn left so the water is on your right side.

Follow the waterway for about 3 miles (but the walk can be shortened if you leave at bridges marked 'x' on the map where the roads lead back to Market Bosworth). At bridge No 44 gain the road and cross the water.

6 Follow the lane to the village of Carlton. There is one signed path on the right which you should ignore. At the next, after ½ mile of road walking, take a path over a stile on the right. Walk over the pasture to a stile. There is now a fenced path – take care of the barbed wire!

7 Follow the waymarked path (yellow arrows and yellow-topped posts again) through fields and by woods. When you reach a farm vehicle way follow it to a road. Turn right to return to Market Bosworth.

resting place on their passages of migration.

The route goes over some arches of the now-obsolete Hemlingford Bridge. Here was once a fording place of the swift-flowing river Tame; in 1783 a public subscription list was opened to raise funds to build the bridge. Nearby is the sad structure of Hemlingford Mill which is crying out for restoration. There has been a mill here as far back as the Domesday Survey of 1086. Now unused, it has been a gun barrel mill, sawmill, paper mill, leather mill, grain-mill and, more latterly, a garden centre.

A slight detour takes you to Kingsbury Hall, now in a state of disrepair but once a grand castle or fortified house. Parts of the curtain wall and arches remain to tell us of past glories. Some authorities suggest that the place may have been occupied by the King of Mercia but the present house is from the late medieval period. The Norman church nearby has a 14th century tower.

The return route uses the towing path of the Birmingham and Fazeley Canal. This waterway is part of the extensive Birmingham Canal Naviga-tions which by the end of the last century was moving nine million tons of cargo each year. The canal is no longer used by commercial craft but is a popular route for holiday craft. There is also, shortly before you turn back for the car park, a waterside inn which enjoyed much trade from the bargees.

THE WALK

1 From the Water Park car park at Bodymoor Heath walk past the vehicle barrier. At a junction of vehicle ways turn left (signed to Far Leys). Within 100 yards take a path right. Pass by a small pool (on the left side) to a meeting of pathways. Turn left to walk over a footbridge to another junction of paths. Turn right.

2 Walk alongside the extensive Pool. Keep ahead on a constant heading to

Walk 6
KINGSBURY WATER PARK
Length : 4½ miles

Hemlingford bridge over the river Tame.

GETTING THERE: From Junction 9 of the M42 take the A4097. Within 2 miles take the road to the entrance to the Water Park at Bodymoor Heath.

PARKING: There is a car park (fee paying) at the Water Park.

MAP: OS Landranger – Birmingham and surrounding area 139 (GR 204960).

Until 1973 the area over which the walk begins was synonymous with the despoilation caused by the extensive extraction over 50 years of sand and gravel from the valley of the river Tame. Half of the pits were left to fill naturally with water; the rest were filled (mainly with waste materials from power stations) and the area sympathetically landscaped by the Warwickshire County Council to create a magnificent water park. Above all, this is a place where nature has been given a prime role. Flowers of the marsh and waterside abound and many birds use the parkland lakes as a

Enjoying a stroll in the ruins of Kingsbury Hall.

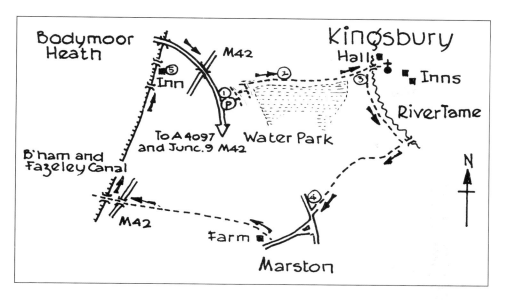

leave the Park along the 'Planks' (a raised causeway above the flood plain). High to the left is the Hall. Cross the bridge over the river Tame and climb the many steps to visit Kingsbury and the church.

3 Retrace your steps over the river. At once turn left. Follow the river to the old bridge and redundant road (now a footpath). Turn right. Follow the way to a main road.

4 Turn left, then soon right to the hamlet of Marston. Go past a little green and junction of roads. A hundred yards further on take a farm road on the right. Go past the farm buildings and continue to the canal bridge. Gain the towing path and continue now walking northwards with the water on your left side.

5 Continue past an inn and lock gates. At the next road bridge leave the towing path. Go under the bridge then climb to the road. Turn left and follow the road back to the entrance to the Water Park.

Walk 7
THE PLEASANT COUNTRYSIDE OF FOUL END
Length : 8 miles

Shustoke Reservoir.

GETTING THERE: Shustoke is 3 miles along the B4114 from the A446 at Coleshill.

PARKING: In the quiet road outside the inn or the car park by the Severn-Trent Water Co. reservoir.

MAP: OS Landranger – Birmingham and surrounding area 139 (GR 227909).

What an unfortunate name is Foul End! This is a quiet corner of Warwickshire which has somehow resisted the sprawl of the city and where agriculture is still paramount. Perhaps that name denotes that Farmer Fowler once tilled the soil!

There were many coal mines hereabouts too but today there are few working mines. Mother Nature has done her best (and succeeded) in clothing the spoil heaps and there is little evidence of the old industry. There are no high hills on the route but a wonderful sense of remoteness in this area, much of which is owned by Sir William Dugdale of Blyth Hall.

Shustoke, where the walk begins, looks modern but the name was recorded at the Domesday Survey of 1086 as Scotscote. The clue to this apparent anomaly is that the village was once sited a mile away from the present centre. In 1650 the region was struck by the Plague and the inhabitants moved, to leave the church isolated with only a few farmsteads clustered around it.

The old centre, passed towards the end of the walk, is now called Church End. The church is on a gentle rise and was sited here in Saxon times. The Normans replaced the building but much of what we see today is the result of the 1887 restoration following a lightning strike and fire.

Shustoke Reservoir has nudged the village since its construction in the 19th century to supply water to Coventry and Nuneaton. The water company encourage visitors to enjoy viewing the waterfowl, use the picnic area and walk the pathways around the shores, and this makes a pleasant end to the walk. Students of architecture enthuse about the Victorian 'cathedral-like' pumphouses and a sailing club also uses the water.

THE WALK

1 Walk along the B4114 towards Coleshill. Just past Castle Lane (on the left) turn right along a signed footpath (beside a vehicle way) on the right. Continue along the firm track. Cross the brook to a meeting of signed paths.

2 Keep ahead over a field to a crossing place of the railway. Still maintain the direction, never far from a railway on the left, to border a field to a stile to a lane. Turn left for a yard or so, then take a path right to regain the old heading.

3 The path is again alongside a left-hand railway then veers right. Just past a 'Warning' notice the path divides. Do not go ahead into woods but turn right over a bridge. At once swing left to again take the former direction alongside a left-hand hedge.

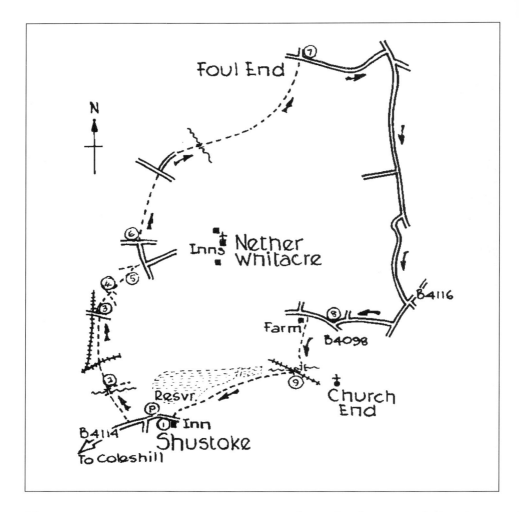

4 Go over another bridge to a bold waymark post and meeting of paths. Keep ahead (still by a left-hand hedge) to another junction of paths. Maintain the direction over a double step stile to cross the field. Climb another double stile and walk over the field to climb yellow-topped stiles and pass through a builder's store yard.

5 Cross a rough vehicle track. In a meadow take the arrowed direction to the far right-hand corner stile. Follow the edge of left-hand hedges to Bakehouse Lane. (To the right and left are delightful timbered cottages.) Turn left to a junction. To the right is Nether Whitacre and its good inn, otherwise keep ahead along Bakehouse Lane.

6 At a T-junction cross to the opposite path and take the arrowed way. Keep

Nether Whitacre.

ahead through fields to a road. Cross to the bridleway signed opposite along a vehicle way. When the houses end keep along the path to a large arable field. Take the indicated direction of the bridleway to walk to the far side. A farm tractor way leads to a lane junction at Foul End.

7 Turn right. At a T-junction proceed right, then bear right at the next junction (signed Over Whitacre). Keep ahead along narrow country lanes. Keep ahead at a junction. At the next junction turn right to the B4116. Turn right, then right again along Pound Lane to the B4098.

8 Turn right. The next path is on the left through a wrought iron gate adjoining ornate gates to a former farmyard. Go through the yard and follow the arrowed direction to a stile in the far right-hand corner of the meadow. Climb further stiles then go left to a footbridge over the brook.

9 Continue to the tunnel under the railway. Follow the path right. The path borders fields and woods on a constant heading to join the vehicle way beside Shustoke Reservoir. Follow the vehicle way back to Shustoke.

THE ROMANS' GREAT HIGHWAY

Length : 8 miles

Shire horses on the route.

GETTING THERE: The start is 5 miles south west of Hinkley along the A5 at the junction with the B577 at High Cross.

PARKING: There is limited parking by the information board at the road junction.

MAP: OS Landranger – Leicester and Coventry 140 (GR 473896).

This is great hunting country for the fields are large and flat, and we are told that they 'are not an easy option for those wishing to walk at speed!' The land is clay and can stick to the boots but here is a quiet and strangely lovely and lonely countryside. Through this landscape ran one of the principal roads of Roman Britain.

The start of the walk is at High Cross which was like the 'spaghetti junction' of the era for here was the meeting of Watling Street with the Fosse Way. At High Cross is a stone monument which has weathered since

1712 but was severely damaged by lightning in 1791. There is a faded Latin inscription which translated reads: 'If Traveller you seek for the footsteps of the ancient Romans, here you may behold them, for here their most celebrated ways, crossing each other, extend to the utmost bourne.'

Here the main route from London (Londinium) to the north at Chester (Deva) met the greatest east-west highway. The Fosse Way took the legionaries from Lincoln (Lindum Colonia) to Bath (Aquae Sulis) and on to the Dorset coast. It was constructed around AD 45 at the start of the Roman occupation of Britain. It is virtually straight for 200 miles. The route is mostly covered by modern roads but here we walk along a section which has survived in something akin to its original form.

There was a busy Roman military station called Venonis on the upland, which is 443 feet above sea level. We too can appreciate the views from this natural vantage point which dominates the surrounding countryside in all directions.

The walk continues through the Fosse Meadows Nature Park, which covers many ancient and undisturbed pastures and is owned by Blaby District Council. There are new plantations of saplings and the park includes woodland and meadow way-marked trails.

At Sharnford, by the river Soar, the route brings you to the first of several attractive villages to be visited; the buildings are from many different periods and styles and therefore have a picturesque beauty. There are timber-framed black and white, brick-rendered (often gleaming white!) and local stone buildings. Fortunately, most of the villages in Leicestershire have retained their inns even if shops and schools have gone. From Claybrooke Parva, country paths bring you back to High Cross.

THE WALK

1 From High Cross go through the kissing gate by the information board. Follow the Fosse Way along the wide grassy cart track. Drop down through a gate and follow the clear track for 1½ miles. When the track becomes a tarmac lane go over a stile on the left.

The weathered memorial stone at High Cross.

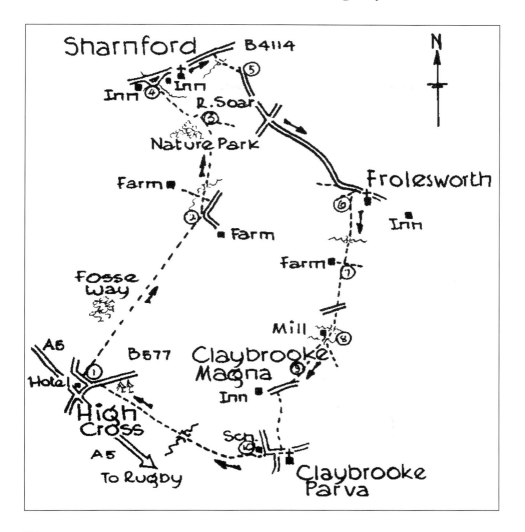

2 Follow the faint path diagonally over the pasture. Climb stiles and cross a farm drive. Continue to a footbridge and cross the brook. Maintain the general heading following the Leicestershire Round waymarks (arrows containing a circle) through the Nature Park. Take care as there are other footpaths signed. The Leicestershire Ring is a 100 mile circular walk around the county devised in 1987 to mark the centenary of the Leicestershire Footpath Association.

3 Go alongside a right-hand border; do not go through a kissing gate (on the right) but continue to a corner gate (seat nearby). Follow the fenced path at the borders of a pasture to a step stile. Continue alongside a cricket field then pick up the side of the little river Soar.

4 Over a stile, turn right along a lane across the river. The lane leads to the main road at Sharnford. Turn right. Climb the hill past the inn and church. A quarter of a mile beyond the church turn right along a well-used footpath. Cross the river and continue to a lane.

5 Turn right towards Frolesworth. Just before the church and opposite the gleaming 'White Cottage' take a path on the right. (Note the path may be unsigned.) Walk along a cart track. Just past a house and dried-up pond (on the left) the cart track swings right.

6 Maintain the old direction, striking out over the open field and aiming just to the right of a farmstead on a far hill. Drop down the valley and cross footbridges. Keep ahead out of the valley to reach the farm drive (to the left of the farm).

7 Still keep the same heading. Follow waymarks through fields and over a bridge. Nearing a lane, pick up a left-hand hedge. Cross the lane and keep the old direction. Over the brow make for a yellow marker post. Pass through a gate which is often overlooked by some fine carthorses in the field on the left.

8 Continue over a bridge and farm drive. (To the right is the 17th century Claybrooke Mill but do respect the privacy of the owner.) Go through a gate ahead and cross a bridge to a field. Walking parallel to the right-hand hedge, make for the yellow markers in an opposite boundary.

9 In the next field maintain the heading to a stile in the top left corner. Walk, right, along Bell Street. Within a hundred yards or so take a signed path left. Go along a vehicle drive, then continue along a well-used path through fields to emerge on the B577 near the church at Claybrooke Parva. Turn right.

10 On a bend in the road is the school. Take a signed path to the left of the school. In a field, turn right to follow the edge of the field. Follow the waymarked path to cross a footbridge. Walking out of the valley aim for the tall fir trees. Go by a protruding corner which juts into our field and climb further waymarked stiles to rejoin the B577. Turn left back to High Cross.

Walk 9
THE BUSY FOOTPATH JUNCTION OF KINVER EDGE

Length : 8 miles

The famous rock houses at Kinver Edge.

GETTING THERE: 3 miles from Stourbridge along the A458 take a road left signed to Kinver. Through the village on the main road towards Cookley take the first lane right. Half a mile past the church turn left at the junction.

PARKING: The car park is reached on the right within ½ mile of turning off at the junction.

MAPS: OS Landranger – Birmingham and surrounding area 139 and Kidderminster and Wyre Forest area 138 (GR 837821).

Kinver Edge is a wood-clothed sandstone ridge which rises to over 500 feet above sea level. The magnificent scarp edge faces towards the west so there are glorious views far over the Severn Valley towards the border hills of Wales. It is a major junction of long-distance foot-paths for here meet the Staffordshire Way, the North Worcestershire Path

FOOD and DRINK

In Kinver there are several good pubs and cafes. In particular, the White Harte, an old coaching inn in the centre of the village offers a large selection of food. The fish and vegetarian dishes are something of a speciality. Telephone: 01384 872305. The George and Dragon in the High Street is popular with locals which is always a good recommendation. Telephone: 01384 872094.

and the Worcestershire Way. It is not surprising that all wanted a share in this beautiful upland!

The walk begins by following the North Worcestershire Path up to the ancient hill fort. Here was a splendid strategic site which commanded a wide area, so it was perhaps inevitable that the Ancient Britons built them-selves a large fortification. We can see

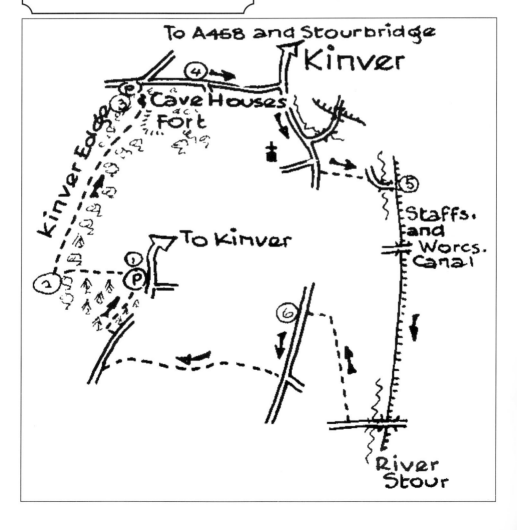

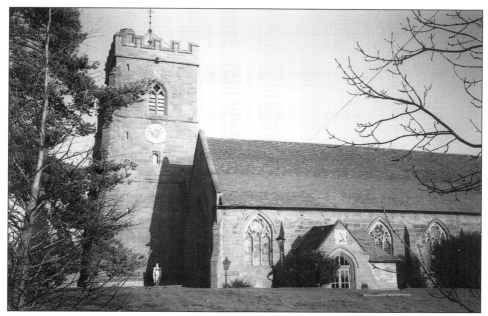

Kinver church.

the banks and ditches marking the extent of the fort, some eleven acres, using the escarpment as a defensive feature.

Almost 300 acres of the high land of the ridge is owned by the National Trust after a gift from the Lee family in 1917. The Edge is famous for the rock houses built into the soft sandstone cliffs. For many hundreds of years these dwellings were happily occupied and indeed in the last centuries many became quite sophisticated and desirable. With modern standards, however, all the inhabitants left; one house became a cafe much loved by walkers. Many of the properties became targets for vandals, but fortunately the National Trust took the matter in hand and in 1993 one was rebuilt for a resident custodian.

After passing the cave houses, the walk descends, via Kinver, to the towing path of the Staffordshire and Worcestershire Canal. The canal was opened in 1772 and was another waterway planned by that great engineer James Brindley. It joins the river Severn at Stourport with the Trent and Mersey Canal and is now a delightful waterway for pleasure cruisers and for walkers along the towing paths.

The walk then returns to the Edge car park through wooded countryside, along another section of the North Worcestershire Path.

THE WALK

1 From the car park walk through a barrier and follow the path signed as the North Worcestershire Path. Follow the waymarked path to the top of the

> ### PLACES of INTEREST
>
> **Kinver** was once an important market town, with much of its industry based on local sheep farms. It was also a staging town on the route between Chester and Worcester with many inns and the associated traders to serve the travellers and the coaches. The church (rather isolated and overlooking the town) dates from the 14th century although Norman work can be seen. There is a rather fine three-decker pulpit which was carved in 1625.

ridge and the junction of the three long distance paths.

2 Turn right. The well-used track runs along the ridge and passes the trig. point and the banks and ditches (on the right) of the hill fort. Pass a toposcope (a wonderful viewpoint) and follow the signs to 'Cave Houses'.

3 Follow the path, which descends around bends and past the cave houses to go to a road. Turn right.

4 Pass and ignore junctions till you come to a main road. Turn right and follow the road through the village. Just past the lane signed right to Kinver church take a signed path left. Walk over the field to a lane. Turn right and cross the river to the canal. Turn right along the towing path.

5 Follow alongside the waterway. At the second road bridge leave the canal. Walk along the road and over the river towards the hamlet of Caunsall. Within a few steps the next path is over a stile on the right. This is the North Worcestershire Path. Follow the waymarked path over the fields to a stile to a road.

6 Turn left. After 500 yards continue right along a signed bridleway. This track is sometimes muddy and after a mile a lane is reached. Turn right. Within 300 yards a path goes into a wood on the left. The path wends its way through the trees back to the car park.

Walk 10
THE LICKEY HILLS – THE UPLANDS OF BIRMINGHAM

Length : 6½ or 2 miles

A welcome seat on the Lickey Hills.

GETTING THERE: Take the A38 south out of Birmingham. At the M5 motorway junction follow the A491. Within a mile take the B4551 right. After just over a mile (opposite Manchester Inn) take a road right to a car park of the Country Park

PARKING: The car park of Waseley Hill Country Park.

MAP: OS Landranger – Birmingham and surrounding area 139 (GR 972783).

The Countryside Act empowered local authorities to create country parks to provide opportunities and facilities for the enjoyment of open air recreation by the public. For many years there was a plan to create such a park around the uplands of Waseley and Windmill Hills on Birmingham's doorstep, to link the areas where for many years the public had already enjoyed the right to freely roam.

To the south the Lickey Hills (which rise to 987 feet on Beacon Hill)

FOOD and DRINK

The cafe at the Visitor Centre is open daily 9 am to 5 pm (in summer) and 11 am to 4 pm in winter. Telephone: 01562 711051. Just off the route near the farm along Chapman's Hill, is the Manchester Inn. This hostelry welcomes walkers – there is a boot-proof tiled floor! Try the cod here – it is something special. Telephone: 01562 710242. There is another inn near Holy Well. An ice-cream van often parks on Beacon Hill.

---

were open to all, ever since there had been angry reaction to illegal encroachment and enclosure under the Act of 1803 which eliminated the commonland. To the north the Clent Hills are safe under the guardianship of the National Trust. The designation of the Waseley Hills Country Park has thus established a virtually unbroken band of green to the west of the city. The old image of a park as an amalgam of formal gardens, pools and trimmed lawns is soon dispelled; here is a place where Nature is allowed to continue to weave its own patterns and the grass is not trimmed by mechanical cutters but by sheep and cattle.

The walk starts by the Leisure Centre of the Country Park. Here one can study charts, maps and information boards to gain local knowledge to enhance the enjoyment of the walk. On Waseley Hill is a toposcope to identify local landmarks.

This exhilarating walk explores this lovely area, climbing to the ancient beacon site. Many of these sites date from the 16th century when the Tudors were concerned about invasion from across the Channel. They have been lit

again in recent times to celebrate Royal anniversaries. The Lickey site now takes the form of a mock stone castle built by young people.

The climbs are quite steep but the rewards are stunning views over the surprisingly chequered green of Birmingham and westwards far over the Worcestershire countryside, with the uplands of Bredon, the Malverns, the Abberley Hills and the Clees on hazy-blue distant horizons.

THE WALK

1   From the car park walk back to the road. Turn left then immediately left again to walk down Chapman's Hill (signed as a no through road). By a farm and as the vehicle way twists sharp right, keep ahead along the bridleway.

2   The track goes through trees and crosses the bed of a stream. Keep ahead along a wide way then pass by a house. Still maintain the direction along a track to meet a junction of ways near a farm (on the right side). Turn left through a gate and climb the rise alongside a left-hand hedge.

PLACES of INTEREST

The route passes near an obelisk erected in 1834 by John Hanson to commemorate the death of Henry Windsor, the eighth Earl of Plymouth. Later on the walk we can see **Chadwich Manor**. The five-bay house dates from the late 17th century. The Manor with its 431 acres was one of the many generous bequests to the public from the Cadbury family and is now under the care of the National Trust, although not open to the general public.

The 'castle' on Beacon Hill.

3 Pass through a gate and keep ahead. (There is a seat here to sit and marvel at the view!) Just beyond a picnic table a junction of ways is reached. For the shorter walk turn left through the kissing gate and follow the path back as described in Point 10. For the full route turn right to drop down to a gate then regain height alongside a left-hand hedge. When this ends maintain the heading.

4 By a wooden fence the waymark arrow directs us left to walk downhill to a kissing gate to the left of a water trough. Beyond, follow the track through trees to a car park. Continue to a lane and turn left to Holy Well. At a junction turn right to cross the A38 main road.

5 At once take a signed bridleway on the right. The bold track leads to a lane. Cross, to either pick up the path going to the right alongside the lane through the bushes, (or alternatively to turn left on the lane to meet the path on your right within a few steps). Follow the path out of the trees to walk (now leaving the side of the lane) over the grass at the top of the scarp edge with the golf course below on the left.

6 At the castle-like beacon site swing right to the car park. On the road turn left. Within 300 yards take a signed path over a fence stile on the right. (The obelisk is further along the road on the right.) Follow the clear path over the pasture. Cross a vehicle drive, then maintain the old heading over further fields to a stile onto a lane.

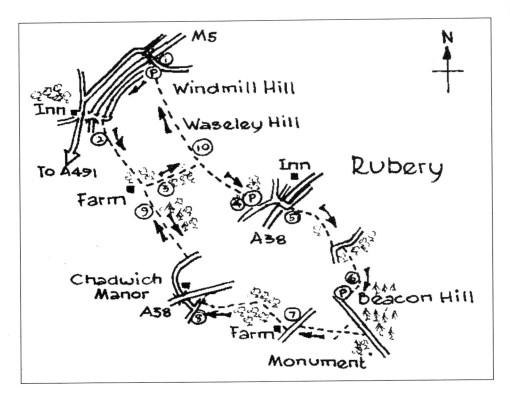

7   Turn left. Within a few steps turn right along a farm vehicle way. Past the farm, keep ahead along a footpath through the trees. This leads to a garden, follow the way ahead along the house drive to a road. Turn left.

8   At a junction go right. The lane passes under the A38 main road (Chadwich Manor is over to the right) then narrows. Past cottages the road starts to climb. Turn left along a farm 'road'. The concrete way goes over a cattle grid. Follow the 'road' to woods. Here leave the vehicle way by climbing a stile to woodlands. Follow the path over another stile to a field.

9   Walk the length of the field to a stile (to the right of a farm) and a meeting of ways where you were earlier on the walk. Turn right up the rise to again walk through the corner gate. Keep ahead to the meeting of ways just past the picnic table.

10   Turn left through the kissing gate. Take the direction up the hill to a distant marker post. (There is a seat here.) Maintain the heading, passing just to the right of a fir wood, and drop down the hill to a gate by the Visitor Centre.

Walk 11
THE ROMANTIC LANDS OF KENILWORTH
Length : 6½ or 3½ miles

Kenilworth Castle.

GETTING THERE: Kenilworth is 7 miles south west of Coventry. From the A429 or A452 follow the Kenilworth Castle signs.

PARKING: By the castle walls at Castle Green (B4103) (not in the main castle car park).

MAPS: OS Landranger – Birmingham and surrounding area 139 and Leicestershire and Coventry area 140 (GR 280723)

The countryside around the castle of Kenilworth is gentle and unspectacular but always has that 'away from it all' remoteness. Apart from that great chunk of sandstone near the Fineham and Inchford brooks, nowhere else on the walk do we have to scale rocks and cliffs – the land is intensively farmed with arable prevailing.

Often arable land means difficult walking, with paths not reinstated after ploughing as the law dictates, but not here. There is a very active footpath

---

FOOD and DRINK

There are inns cheek by jowl at the start at Castle Green. The Queen and Castle is part of the Beefeater chain; the food may be a little predictable but offers excellent value with the Mr Men menu for hungry youngsters. Telephone: 01926 852661. Nearby is the Clarendon Arms, (telephone: 01926 852017) which is a more humble pub with the boast that 'the burgers are the best in Warwickshire'. About halfway along the route is the Tipperary Inn with its association with the famous song. It has a good wide menu for a country inn. Telephone: 01676 533224.

---

preservation society which liaises with landowners to ensure rights of way are clear and a pleasure to use.

The walk takes you away from the castle towards Meer End, passing 16th century Rudfyn Manor on the way. At Meer End is the Tipperary Inn. It was called the Plough when it was the home of Harry Williams, who with Jack Judge wrote the famous First World War song.

The landscape on the homeward leg of the walk has been fashioned by man; Henry V did not greatly like the grand apartments at the castle and built a pavilion called The Pleasance some ½ mile away. This was surrounded by two moats and connected to a vast lake by a deep cutting along which the state barges could travel to the isolated retreat.

The lake itself was man-made by damming the two brooks near the castle; today cattle graze over the rich pastures which are overlooked on the route but your return path cuts straight across the site of The Pleasance. Ridges and hollows still mark the extent of the pavilion, but where monarchs dallied rabbits now play.

Although much of the walk is over fields which are now tilled you pass many pools which indicate they were once grazing lands for cattle. There is also a meandering path through the delightful Poors Wood – a pleasant mixture of deciduous and coniferous trees under which is a carpet of bluebells in springtime.

THE WALK

1   From the car park walk along the path with the great castle walls on the left. Climb the stile to a large rough pasture. Turn right to climb a stile to a vehicle track called Purlieu Lane by a cottage capped by thatch. Turn left.

2   Cross the brook and immediately take a signed path on the right. Over the stile, walk the clear path over the field to pass through a metal gate just

---

PLACES of INTEREST

The walk starts at **Kenilworth Castle**. It was in 1125 that the Chief Justice and Treasurer to Henry I, Geoffrey de Clinton, decided that the sandstone rock hereabouts would make an ideal and worthy site for his home. The next Henry liked the place too and (50 years after Clinton's construction) he added the massive keep. King John's contribution was great with an expenditure of £2,000. John of Gaunt, the Duke of Lancaster, set about improving the castle and his additions changed the place from its former fierce, fortress-like structure. It became a ruin when it was 'slighted', by blowing up parts of it, by the Parliamentarians during the Civil War.

The Tipperary Inn passed on the route.

to the left of ruined animal shelters. Two paths are signed here; take the left-hand path which crosses diagonally over the field to a far stile.

3   Follow the path on much the same direction over further fields to a farm lane by a red-brick cottage. For the shorter walk turn left to the point marked 'x' on the map. For the longer route take the next path (signed Meer End) over a stile almost opposite. Walk at the head of a large arable field to a stile into a small wood.

4   Follow the arrowed way to the next field and walk alongside a left-hand hedge to pass through another small wood. Maintain the heading over the open field and pass through a hedge gap. Keep ahead over an arable field to a hedge. Turn left; within 250

yards and by a pool swing right through a hedge gap.

5   Follow the right-hand hedge of a field. Pass through a corner gap and turn left to walk under electricity lines. At a marker post turn right to go over the open field, now aiming towards buildings. Pass a jutting corner to another corner, where you turn right alongside a left-hand hedge. Within 75 yards go through a gap on the left to a vehicle drive.

6   Turn left, then right by the gates of Rudfyn Manor. Follow the edge of the field to a distant corner. Go left through scrubland to the next field. Regain the old heading (right-hand hedge) to pass through a metal gate (the stile is obsolete). There are two arrows here; take the direction of the left-hand one to go

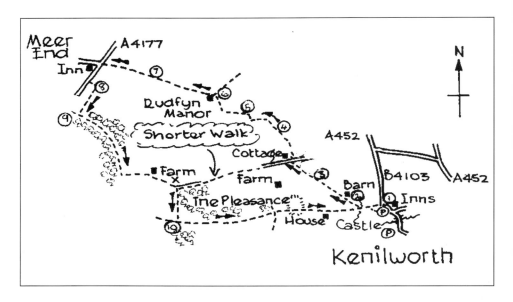

over the field to a stile in the middle of the far hedge.

7 Over two stiles keep by a right-hand hedge. Go through a metal hunting gate. Keep ahead. Over stiles by a pool bear left towards a bungalow. Over a stile join a drive to the main road by the Tipperary Inn. Turn left. Within 200 yards and opposite Tipperary Cottage take a signed path left. At the end of a fenced way go over a stile right.

8 The path is now waymarked at the sides of several fields and crossing vehicle drives. By a small barn go left, then right to regain the old heading. At a drive by house gates again go left, then right through a metal kissing gate. Keep ahead to a T-junction of tracks by a wood. Turn left (blue arrow).

9 Follow the clear track through the wood, keeping ahead at other tracks, to follow the head of an arable field. Pass through a corner gap. Turn left along a tractor way to farm buildings. Pass to the right to join the drive. Follow this to a wood. (Point marked 'x' on the map for the shorter walk.) Turn right. (The trees are now on the left.) At the bottom of the slope turn left.

10 Keep ahead along a waymarked path to pass through The Pleasance site. Climb a stile and continue ahead to join a vehicle way which becomes Purlieu Lane. Maintain the heading and retrace your steps to the car park.

Walk 12
THE MAGNIFICENT HOUSES AND GARDENS OF PACKWOOD AND BADDESLEY CLINTON
Length : 7 miles

Packwood House.

GETTING THERE: 8 miles along the A4177 and A4141 north of Warwick turn left along a lane at Baddesley Clinton then left again at a junction. Within a mile is a car park and picnic site at Hay Wood.

PARKING: The car park at Hay Wood.

MAP: OS Landranger – Birmingham and surrounding area 139 (GR 205711).

The gentle countryside in this part of Warwickshire would originally have been part of the vast Forest of Arden. There are no high hills and in spite of being near large conurbations, it retains a very rural ambiance. There are still small pockets of woodland with old oaks.

The walk begins through Hay Wood – a mixed wood with deciduous trees and new pines. It has a fine bridleway wending a way through it and is especially attractive at springtime when the bluebells scent the air. The soils here are gravelly and therefore not ideal for agriculture.

The two great houses visited on this walk are under the care of the National Trust. Packwood has splendid gardens but the real gem here is the topiary work depicting the Sermon on the Mount. The yews were first planted by John Fetherston about 1700.

Packwood House is open from April to September and is a romantic house containing a wealth of French and Flemish tapestries. Besides the renowned clipped yews the garden includes a colourful terraced herbaceous border and a stroll around the lake is a delight. Telephone: 01564 782024.

Baddesley Clinton Hall is a romantically sited medieval moated manor house that has changed little since 1634. It is approached by a creeper-clad Queen Anne bridge and is open from March to October on Wednesday to Sunday and bank holiday Mondays. Telephone: 01564 783294. There are

many secret hiding places to delight youngsters; one was built by the expert hide builder Nicholas Owen below the level of the moat. The church nearby has a tower which was built by Nicholas Brome to expiate his crime – he had killed a priest.

Canalside walking adds greatly to the pleasure of this ramble. For a mile after leaving Packwood House the route is along the towing path of the Stratford-upon-Avon Canal, passing the locks of the Lapworth flight. This waterway covers 25 miles and was fully opened in 1816 to convey coal southwards and lime in the opposite direction. The Grand Union Canal, formed by an amalgamation of many waterways in 1929, is joined twice on the walk, the second time on the return route which brings you back towards Baddesley Clinton Hall and church.

THE WALK

1 Out of the car park turn right along the lane. Just past the drive to Baddesley church (on the left) turn right down a vehicle way. Go past the Keeper's Cottage and enter the woods.

2 Follow the main path through Hay Wood, going over crossing paths to a stile to a field. Cross the field towards a farmstead. Go between buildings to join the drive to the main road.

3 Turn left along the A4141. Take care for ¾ mile. Almost opposite the drive to Warren Farm turn left down a vehicle way. At the end go over a stile. Keep at the edge of fields to a lane. Turn left. (The convent is nearby.)

Ramblers at Baddesley Clinton church.

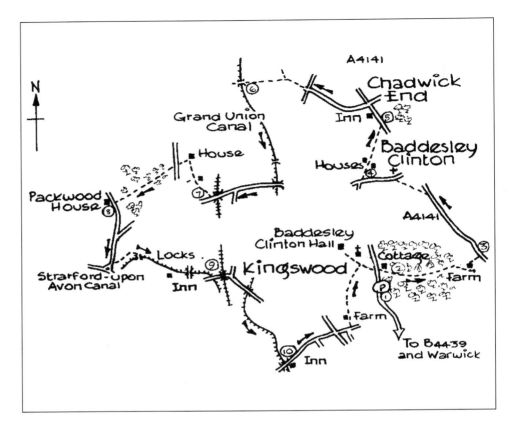

4 Within 200 yards take a path signed on the right along a house drive. (This is the Heart of England Way.) Go past barns. The waymarked path is now through fields to a stile to the main road at Chadwick End.

5 Turn left, then left again (Netherwood Lane) at a crossroads. Follow the lane to the junction with Arbour Tree Lane. Cross to the vehicle way opposite. Within 400 yards there is a stile to a meadow. Walk along the field border to the canal bridge.

6 Gain the towing path and walk southwards with the Grand Union Canal on your left side. Leave the canal at the next road bridge. Walk along the road. Pass a junction and cross a railway. At once take a signed path right.

7 Follow the path at the back of houses and along a vehicle way to a lane. Cross to the signed path over a stile almost opposite. The path is along an avenue and direct to a gate onto a lane by Packwood House. Turn left.

8 Walk ahead at a junction. By the next junction take a signed path down a farm drive left. Go past farm build-

9 At the next bridge gain the road (B4439) at Kingswood. Go under the railway to another canal. Gain the towing path and walk southwards with the water on the left.

10 At the next road bridge leave the waterway. Go over the canal and pass an inn. At a crossroads go straight over. Within 300 yards take a signed path on the left. The path borders fields, then is fenced to a vehicle way. Just to the left is Baddesley Clinton church and Hall, but turn right to complete the walk. At a lane turn right to return to the car park.

ings to the Stratford-upon-Avon Canal. Turn left to walk along the towing paths beside locks of the Lapworth flight. Go under a road bridge.

Walk 13
PASTORAL COUNTRY AROUND ALVECHURCH
Length : 5½ miles

The delightful countryside around Alvechurch.

GETTING THERE: Alvechurch is 11 miles south east of Birmingham along the A441.

PARKING: Quiet roadsides in the centre of Alvechurch.

MAP: OS Landranger – Birmingham and surrounding area 139 (GR 028727).

Here are gentle hills from which small brooks tumble and small pockets of woodland in fine mixed terrain. One of the brooks crossed on the walk is the infant river Arrow, which further downstream powered many of the mills used by the old traditional needle industry of Redditch.

It is sometimes difficult on this walk in pleasant green countryside to realise that the borders of Birmingham are only a mile or so distant. There is mainly dairy farming but this is also commuter-land and you are more than likely to see sporting horses in the meadows.

Alvechurch is quite a large village but it has recently been by-passed so some peace has now returned. The centre has some splendid examples of typical Worcestershire black and white timber-framed buildings. Some of these date from the 16th century. The place was once the site of a bishop's moated summer palace, but the reason they selected Alvechurch for their holiday retreat 700 years ago is now lost in antiquity. The palace, by the river, is today marked only by the outlines of the moat and fish ponds.

Early on in the walk we go by the large Newbourne Wood, a nature reserve owned and managed by the Worcestershire Nature Conservation Trust. Then country lanes and meadows take the route to follow the Roman road of Ryknild Street, along which the legionaries marched from the Fosse Way at Stow-on-the-Wold to their station at Wall on Watling Street near Lichfield. Ryknild Street is a deep lane, banked and topped by a hedge which reminds one of Devon. The return to Alvechurch is through gentle farmland.

THE WALK

1 From the square in the middle of Alvechurch cross to the black and

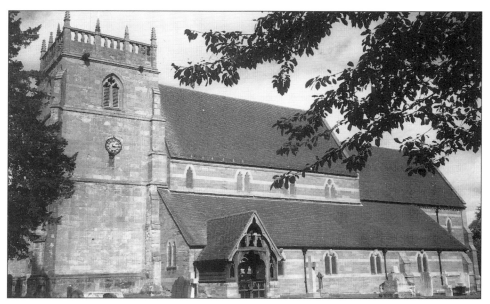

Alvechurch church.

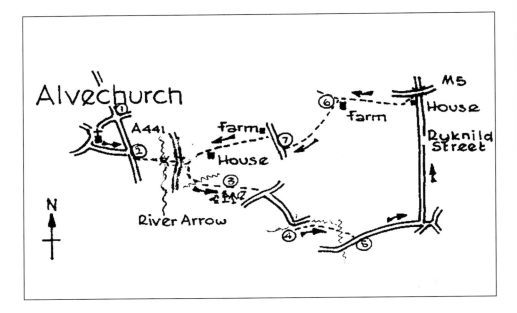

white buildings and continue along Bear Hill. At the top of the hill turn left along a lane signed as a no through road. The lane twists right by the drive to the church. Continue to the main road.

2 Turn right, then at once left. The bridleway is signed through a gateway and along a farm drive. You go over the river Arrow and under the by-pass. There is soon a path branching off to the right and this is the way. The well-used path climbs through meadows then borders Newbourne Wood.

3 The path becomes a tractor way which you follow to a road at Rowney Green. Cross to Gravel Pit Lane which descends steeply. As the lane twists 90 degrees left keep ahead. The path goes to the right-hand side of a white cottage and its garden to a stile and bridge over a brook.

4 In the meadow turn left. Follow the waters of the brook downstream at the borders of meadowland to a stile and bridge. Recross the water and in the

---

PLACES of INTEREST

The village of **Alvechurch** is a place to linger awhile. The church has a dedication to St Lawrence and the name of the village is derived from the possible founder of the church, Aelfgytn (an Anglo-Saxon). The church, on the traditional high land (to be nearer heaven!), was largely rebuilt by a Victorian restorer named Butterfield. He literally 'raised the roof'; the low 15th century tower escaped interference so the building now has a rather unbalanced appearance. There is a rather fine stained glass window which commemorates the Coronation in 1837 of Queen Victoria. There is also a Norman doorway, and a tomb depicting an armour-clad knight of the 1189 crusade.

pasture (where there are signs of medieval ridge and furrow strip farming) bear right to a stile onto a lane.

5 Turn left to a junction. Turn left along Ryknild Street. Just before the motorway bridge turn left. The bridleway is signed along a farm drive. On reaching the farm (a horse riding centre) go through gates to keep the house on your left.

6 Do not follow the main drive but continue through gates to follow the bridleway, to soon pass a large new barn. Join a farm drive and continue to a lane.

7 Turn right for a few steps then go left. The bridleway is signed along a farm drive. Keep ahead, with the farm buildings on the right, to go through gates to a fenced farm vehicle way. Follow this past a house. Walk along the vehicle drive to join the outward route. Retrace your steps to the main road and Alvechurch.

Walk 14
HENLEY AND THE CASTLE OF THE DE MONTFORTS
Length : 6 miles

The castle site above Beaudesert.

GETTING THERE: Henley-in-Arden is 13 miles south of Birmingham along the A3400.

PARKING: Streetside in the High Street. The walk begins near the church.

MAP: OS Landranger – Stratford-upon-Avon and the surrounding area 151 (GR 151660).

To the east of Henley is the typical Warwickshire countryside of Arden – gentle hills, plenty of ancient hedgerows to foster myriad worlds of nature, narrow banked lanes and small pockets of woodland to remind us of the old Forest which

Shakespeare knew. 'And this life, exempt from public haunt, finds tongues in trees, books in the running brooks, sermons in stones and good in everything; I would not change it', the Bard wrote of Arden in *As You Like It.*

This is agricultural country but not

FOOD and DRINK

The mile-long High Street has many inns and cafes (some with French, Chinese and Indian cuisine). On the route is the Crab Mill Inn at Preston Bagot and the Haven Tea Rooms by the canal. The inn is open all day and vegetarians and children (with their Charlie Chalk Menu (lots of chips!) are well catered for. Telephone: 01926 843342. The tea rooms are licensed and offer a very full menu including cream teas. Telephone: 01926 842420.

the vast prairie variety of some areas. Here there are small farmsteads of mixed farming; there are little fields and plenty of meadows where wild flowers are still allowed to thrive and grazing horses are pleased to see the walker.

Henley-in-Arden is the starting place – but is a town full of delights to delay your departure. The church overlooks the town; St John's dates from the 15th century. Next door is the Guild House where folk from the town have met for over 500 years. Nearby is the Market Cross. The High Street of Henley is a mile long and is a delicious amalgam of building styles throughout the centuries.

Over the tiny river Alne is Beaudesert, which is older than Henley. It was here that the valuable right to hold markets and fairs was given to Thurstane de Montfort by King Stephen. St Nicholas' church here has a magnificent carved Norman doorway.

Above Beaudesert the walk route climbs The Mount, the hill on which the great castle of the de Montforts was

perched. It was mainly built of wood so only ridges and hollows today mark the breezy upland site.

There is another fine church to be seen on the route at Preston Bagot. The Norman All Saints' church with its tower of wooden shingles is on an isolated hilltop but is lovingly maintained. The manor house of Preston Bagot is a solid timber-framed and brick structure and dates from the 16th century. Manor houses abounded in this area – the outlines of another can be seen in the meadow after leaving the canal.

Through this delightful landscape runs the sinuous Stratford-upon-Avon Canal which is a favourite waterway for inland sailors (see Places of Interest). After leaving the towing path the peaceful river Alne brings you back to Henley.

PLACES of INTEREST

The **Stratford-upon-Avon Canal** (opened in 1816) was considered of such importance for the heritage of our land that it was saved from total abandonment in 1960; the National Trust took over responsibility after years of campaigning by enthusiasts led by David Hutchings. This narrow waterway has many interesting aspects. Look out for the barrel-shaped roofs of the lock-keeper's cottage. Some say that the unusual design was the lasting mark of Dutch workers; others think that bridge templates were used to fashion the distinctive shape. Also note the slots down the middle of the bridges to enable horses to change from one tow path to the other side without the necessity of unhitching the craft.

The Stratford-upon-Avon canal.

THE WALK

1   By the church in the High Street of Henley-in-Arden walk along Beaudesert Lane (marked as a no through road). Cross the river. By the church the lane twists sharp right. Keep ahead through a metal kissing gate. Two paths are signed; keep ahead to walk up the steep slopes of the Mount.

2   Keep ahead over the hummocks. Drop down a deep valley then climb up the clear path on the far side. At the top of the hill two paths are signed. Over a stile take the right-hand way through a pasture. Keep just to the right of overhead electricity lines to reach a stile to a lane.

3   Turn left. Pass a vehicle way (path sign). As the lane twists sharply left, keep ahead. The path is signed through a gate and along a house drive. Nearing the house, climb a stile and walk alongside the garden. Keep ahead to climb a stile to a meadow by a barn. Keep the heading to the middle of the meadow then turn 90 degrees left to a stile.

4   Keep the same general heading through further fields with stiles and waymarks to show the way. Nearing a farm climb a corner fence stile, then go over a plank bridge and step stile. Pass to the right of the barn and farm to a gate onto a lane at Preston Bagot.

5   Cross to the opposite path through a kissing gate. Climb the steep hill to the church and continue to a lane. Cross to the path signed opposite. Follow the direction of the arrow to drop down to a bridge over a brook and the Stratford-upon-Avon Canal.

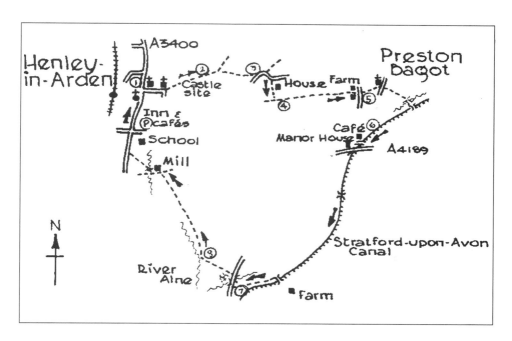

Cross the water and turn right along the towing path.

6 Go by locks and a cottage. By the bridge numbered 47 gain the road through a kissing gate. Turn right then at once left to regain the canal towing path. Pass under a road bridge then cross the waterway. Continue along the towing path now with the water on the left side. Stay by the canal for about another 1¼ miles. At a bridge gain the farm drive and turn right.

7 As you continue to a road look for the manor house site in meadows on the right. On the road turn right. Cross a brook and pass osier beds (willows) on the left. Climb a stile into cow pastures and take the arrowed direction to a stile in the far right-hand corner.

8 The languid river Alne is met here. Follow the river upstream at the side of fields to the drive of Blackford Mill. It is now a private house. Cross the drive and keep the mill building on the right. Go over the water and continue to a sports field. Take the waymarked direction over the field to the A3400. Turn right to return to Henley.

Walk 15
TO LUDLOW - FOR FOSSILS AND A NORMAN CASTLE
Length : 7 miles

Ludlow Castle and the river Teme.

GETTING THERE: Ludlow is near the southern border of Shropshire on the junction of the A49 and A4117.

PARKING: Streetside or in the car park off Market Square.

MAP: OS Landranger – Kidderminster and Wyre Forest area 138 (GR 511746).

Ludlow is situated on the river Teme – the name is from the old British derivation 'dark river' and is the same root as many other rivers such as the Thames, Tame, Tamar and Tavy. Above the fast-flowing waters the town rises spectac-ularly to the Norman castle (see Places of Interest).

Even higher than the castle at 135 feet is the tower of the 15th century parish church of St Laurance. It is one of the largest parish churches in the land; be sure to see the east window which depicts the life of the saint in 27 scenes which feature 300 figures. The ashes of the poet A. E. Housman (who so loved the county of Shropshire) were scattered in the churchyard.

The route starts by walking down Broad Street to the hump-backed Ludford Bridge. The thoroughfare is a wonderful amalgam of Georgian and timber-framed façades and goes under Broad Gate, the only remaining gateway of the seven which once protected the town. The upper part of the street ends at the traditional centre of the town which is the Butter Cross of 1744. The Feathers Hotel is one of the best examples of 17th-century half-timbered buildings in England.

To the south east of Ludlow, where the walk continues, are the vast woodlands which cover some 8,400 acres of the Mortimer Forest. There are deep valleys and high wood-clothed uplands which rise to 900 feet at Mary Knoll, so there are wonderful views. You may spot the herds of fallow deer which roam the woods although they can be elusive; early morning is the best time to try and see them. The rare long-haired deer are descendants of the animals hunted in these parts by the Saxons.

The Forestry Commission planted vast areas of fast-growing coniferous trees; the pines are sweet smelling and have a wonderful aroma after rain. The old deciduous woodlands provided the charcoal burners with their fuel. This industry continued until the 1940s.

The rocky cliff faces in the woods are favourite haunts for fossil hunters. Rocks are chipped away to reveal the shapes of strange creatures which roamed in the shallow sedimentary seas millions of years ago. For many years the youth hostel near the medieval bridge at Ludlow, over which you return to the town, has had a wonderful collection of fossils found in the area.

The famous Feathers Hotel, Ludlow.

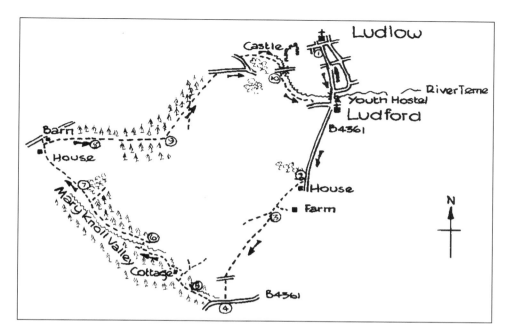

THE WALK

1 From the Butter Cross walk downhill to cross the river Teme at Ludford Bridge. Keep ahead, climbing uphill along the B4361. Within ½ mile at a house on the right called Mabbits Barn a path is signed. Walk a few steps along the drive.

2 The way divides. Take the main left-hand fork with the house away to the left. Keep ahead; the way becomes a track to a stile by a gate. Maintain the direction at the head of an often arable field. Walk along a green track. Go past a farm 'road' (Ludlow sign). A hundred yards further on the track divides.

3 Walk ahead; the path is signed beside the hedge. Climb a stile and keep on the same heading (the hedge is now on the right side). Still keep ahead over further stiles and along field-edge paths to reach a vehicle way. Continue to a road.

4 Turn right. As the road bears left keep ahead along a forest 'road'. You pass through a barrier where there is a forestry notice. There is a brook on the right side. When the 'road' divides take the left-hand way. You now walk along the Mary Knoll valley, never far from the right-hand brook.

5 At a meeting of ways take the right-hand fork. By a cottage the main 'road' twists right by a cliff face. Take the path on the left signed as a 'permissive' path. Again follow the brook which is crossed to reach a forest 'road'. Turn right. After ⅓ mile there is a meeting of 'roads'.

6 Go right to recross the brook then at once left to resume following the brook (now on the left side). Note – From the main road to this point there are many paths and tracks but the general direction is along the valley. When the right-hand trees change from pine to deciduous the main track swings right. Keep ahead (so leaving the main track) to walk along a footpath with the brook still in a deep gulley on the left side.

7 Go through a gate to pastureland. Keep ahead along a fenced way to climb out of the valley to pass through another gate. Turn right. Go past a cottage (on the left). Just before a road swing right to walk by a barn. Go through a gate to a bold tractor way climbing uphill.

8 Pass through a gate and along a fenced track to a gate. Your bridleway is the clear track to the left of the gate. The path goes through an area of cleared forest. Keep ahead on the main track to a forest 'road' and the meeting of many ways. Keep ahead along a stony path.

9 At the end of the woods the path swings left (with an electrical substation on the left). Follow the clear track at the edge of trees (with meadows on the right). At a lane turn right, then left at a junction. Within 400 yards take a path right. The path descends steeply down steps to a bridge over the river. Do not cross.

10 Turn right along a made-up pathway which borders the river. Climb stone steps to a road. Turn left to the B4361. Turn left to retrace your steps over the bridge to the start.

Walk 16
QUIET WAYS WHICH INSPIRED ELGAR
Length : 5 miles

The Teme valley.

GETTING THERE: 3 miles west along the A44 from Worcester turn right at Crown East. Upper Broadheath is a mile along the lane.

PARKING: There is a car park at the Elgar Museum adjoining the Plough Inn.

MAP: OS Landranger – Worcester, The Malverns and surrounding area 150 (GR 807556).

Some of the most evocative music of the English countryside was written by Sir Edward Elgar. He was truly a son of Worcestershire and spent many years in the county, being born at Upper Broadheath and buried at Little Malvern. Elgar loved to explore the rural ways (especially over the Malvern Hills and along the country lanes) on his bicycle and on foot.

This walk starts at the humble cottage in Upper Broadheath which was his birthplace; we can only surmise that the great composer went along the very same byways that we travel on this short ramble. The landscape is so typically English – mixed farms where cattle and sheep graze the meadows, arable lands, small deciduous woods, meandering brooks and wide valleys. Sadly, orchards (marked on the maps) have been rooted out!

About half-way along the route is a delightful lane and bridleway. This runs along the top of the escarpment with the flat river plain of the Teme below. Note in the meadows the water courses marked by a pattern of reeds.

You pass by several old farmsteads; one on the return route includes a building which was once an oast house (where hops were dried), reminding us that these were once great hop-growing areas.

THE WALK

1 There is a signed bridleway alongside Elgar's Cottage and this is your way. The wide track twists around the borders of fields.

2 Pass through a bridle gate to join a vehicle way. Within a few yards is a junction of tractor ways. Turn right. Soon pass right-hand woods then continue to a lane. Turn left to the A44.

3 Turn right to pass the Victorian church at Crown East. Within 250 yards turn left along a school drive signed as a bridleway. After about 200 yards leave the drive. Take the signed bridleway through a metal barrier on the right and over the meadow, aiming just to the left of fir trees.

4 Pass through a metal gate and bearing slightly left, walk just to the right of a pool. Continue to a gate and bridge over a brook to pass between two small woods. In an arable field go left around the border. Within a few steps regain the old direction over the open field. Swing left around an electricity pole to a gate to a main road.

5 Turn right. Within 200 yards turn right along the lane signed Otherton Lane. This high road runs along the ridge top. When the lane twists sharp right, keep ahead. The bridleway is signed through a gate.

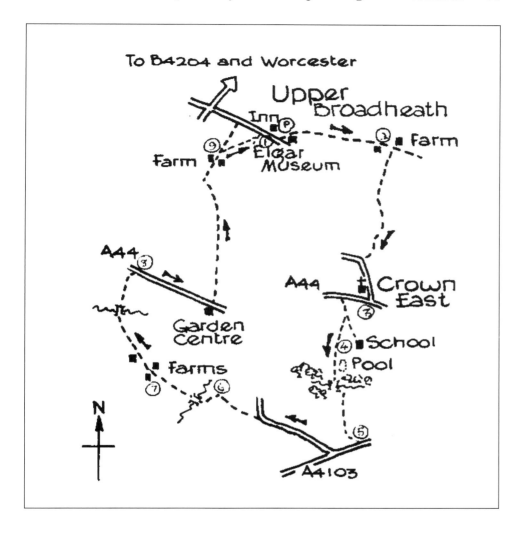

6 Stay on the bridleway which twists left then right through a gate (way-mark arrow here). One hundred yards further on the main track turns 90 degrees left. Keep the old direction to go through a gateway (no gate) and over a brook. Pass through a gate and walk along a sunken way and through a wooden gate. Head towards barns.

7 Join a vehicle way to pass farm buildings (including the old oast house). Keep along the vehicle way to a main road.

8 Turn right. Within 1⅓ mile and opposite the entrance to a garden centre, take a bridleway on the left. Go through a metal gate and walk at the left-hand side of a pasture. Go through a corner gate to a fenced track. Nearing a farm go through a gate on the right to a pasture. Aiming towards a farm-house, go through a gate and pass to the left of the house (with barns on the left).

9 Join the drive. A few yards past the barns climb a stile on the right. In the pasture walk alongside the right-hand hedge to climb a corner stile. Bear left to go through a gate in the far diagonal corner. Continue to a stile to a house drive. Turn left to a road. The starting point is to the right.

Walk 17
HARBURY AND THE LAND OF THE PEYTOS
Length : 6½ miles

The view from Chesterton watermill.

GETTING THERE: 5 miles south east of Leamington Spa along the A425 turn right along the B4452 to Harbury.

PARKING: Along the quiet roadsides in Harbury or in the car park by the sports field.

MAP: OS Landranger – Stratford-upon-Avon and surrounding area 151 (GR 374600).

The countryside to the west of Harbury is redolent with reminders of the Peyto family, although their great mansion at the village of Chesterton was destroyed in 1802 after the family line ended. The Peytos came over with William the Conqueror and lived in this countryside from the 14th century. They were very prominent people in their time, among them Members of Parliament, soldiers and lawyers. During the days of the Civil War Sir Edward Peyto was on the side of the Parliamentarians and helped defend Warwick Castle against the Royalists.

On a gentle hill early in the walk is a distinctive windmill. The tower supported on six stone arches was built (probably by Inigo Jones to the instructions of Sir Edward Peyto) in 1632. The interior of the windmill is open periodically when one can see the cap and giant sails rotated into the wind by a hand-operated winch. Telephone Warwickshire County Council on 01926 410410 for details. Not far away is Chesterton watermill (not open to the public).

The landscape on this walk is mainly arable farmland but meadows do cover the site of the 8 acre Roman encampment on the Fosse Way, halfway along the walk. (In fact the Romans named Chesterton – from 'castra' an encampment and 'ton' a settlement.) Some say that these places are still as remote as when the legionaries trod the hills – unfortunately not true! Modern traffic speeds along the straight highway.

Leaving the Roman station, the route bends south towards Chesterton. There was once a moated manor house among the buildings clustered around the 12th century church but the village was struck twice by the plague by the end of the Middle Ages. The population therefore moved to the present place by the Green leaving the splendid church isolated.

Besides the memorials in Chesterton church, other local reminders of the Peytos include the gateway in the churchyard. Carefully renovated recently, it provided a suitable entry for the family when they came to church. On the route we pass the tall brick wall which surrounded the kitchen garden of the great mansion, before turning back for Harbury.

FOOD and DRINK

Harbury has many inns along its old streets. The building housing the Shakespeare is 500 years old and is a cosy pub with log fires and plenty of quiet nooks and crannies. Like many English hostelries the steak and kidney pies are said to be the best! Telephone: 01926 612357. The Old New Inn passed early on the route provides an excellent Sunday roast. Telephone: 01926 614023.

The Peyto gateway at Chesterton church.

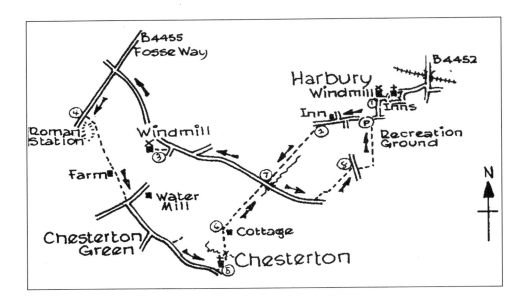

PLACES of INTEREST

Although the focus of this walk is on Chesterton, **Harbury** is of interest too. This place has the tower of a more workaday windmill which lost its sails in recent times. The village was long ago the home of the Wagstaffs who in 1611 founded a school near the 13th century church. It is said a ghostly figure in a frock coat hurries across the road from the school to the church! Harbury was once owned by the Knights Templar, which is remembered at the edge of the village called Temple End.

THE WALK

1 From the centre of Harbury and the church go along Chapel Street (off the road to Warwick). At the end turn right along Park Lane to soon pass an inn. At the end of the village (Temple End) a path starts over a stile on the left.

2 Walk at the side of the field and climb a stile in a corner. Keep ahead near the borders of fields to a stile to a road. Turn right. Keep ahead at a junction. At the next junction turn left. At once go right through a gate and walk over the open field to the windmill.

3 Retrace your steps to the road. Turn left, then again left to walk to the Fosse Way, Turn left. Within ¼ mile go through a gateway left. This is a bridleway beside the Roman station, but the sign on the gatepost may be overgrown.

4 Walk directly away from the road. The track then bears right to become a tractor way. Follow this past the farm and continue to a gate to a road. Cross directly over (signed Chesterton). At a junction (the Green) keep ahead along a lane signed as a no through road to Chesterton church.

5 Go through a gate to the churchyard and keep to the right of the church to a gateway into pastureland. Take the direction indicated to a bridge over the brook. In a large field walk diagonally towards a cottage and a gate in a far corner.

6 Walk around the cottage (keeping it on your right and going through a gate) Walking away from the cottage the bridleway is never far from right-hand field borders. In a far corner go through a bridle gate and over a bridge to a lane.

7 Turn right. Within ½ mile (as the road bends left) go over a stile on the left. Walk by a left-hand hedge. After 100 yards climb a stile and continue alongside right-hand hedges to a lane.

8 Turn right, then at once left over a stile. Walk over the open field past an oak tree. Turn left over a stile to a sports field. Walk the length of the field to a road at Harbury, and back to your starting point.

Walk 18
MEANDERING ON THE MALVERNS
Length : 7 miles or 5 miles

The Malverns.

GETTING THERE: From Malvern go southwards along the A449 through Malvern Wells. At Little Malvern the road divides. Go right to keep along the A449.

Climb the hill to the car park near the junction with the B4232.

PARKING: In the car park (fee paying)

MAP: OS Landranger – Worcester, The Malverns and surrounding area 150 (GR 763404).

T
he traveller Celia Fiennes many years ago described the Malverns as the 'English Alps'. Whilst this may be a trifle too imaginative, approaching the ridge from the east the slopes do look mountainous, dark and mysterious rising from the low-land Worcestershire plain.

The name Malvern is derived from the Welsh 'moel' meaning bare, to which is added 'bryn', a hill. The folds of hard volcanic rock date from the pre-Cambrian period and are some of the oldest in the land. These are often multi-hued showing quartz, mica and felspar. The glistening stones may have

---

FOOD and DRINK

There is a bar at the Malvern Hills Hotel at Wynds Point near the start of the walk which offers a good range of snacks with the home-made soups, assorted jacket potatoes and generously filled sandwiches, being especially good. Children are welcome in the Peter Pocket Room. Telephone: 01684 540237. In the summer months there is a refreshment kiosk opposite the car park.

---

fooled some folk in the past for the northern Malverns still have signs pointing a way to a gold mine!

There is a fine mixture of countryside on this exhilarating walk. After dropping down from the hills the route borders Castlemorton Common. This wide open space is of great interest to the botanist; rare plants thrive here on land which has remained virtually undisturbed (especially from modern farming methods) through many centuries.

A lovely pool, on the route of the shorter walk, was once a stone quarry. Now this has many species of fish; wildfowl love the waters and on the steep cliffs birds find a ready habitat.

On the return leg there is a path through the parkland of Eastnor. Deer roam over the grasslands of the castle grounds – this is a Norman-style 'fortification' but has seen no battles as it is a 'sham' from the 19th century. The obelisk in the grounds of Eastnor Castle is a landmark for miles and was built in limestone (rather than the hard local rock) in 1812 by Lord Somers in memory of his son, who was killed fighting with Wellington in Spain.

The ridge next climbed has a ditch and banks. This is Red Earl's Dyke.

The Earl of Gloucester resolved in 1242 to precisely mark the boundary of the lands disputed with his neighbour, the Bishop of Hereford. The route passes places for those with imaginative minds. There is Hangman's Hill where sheep stealers paid their ultimate penalty and Giant's Cave (seemingly the home of a rather diminutive example of the species!).

The hills rise to 1,394 feet at the Worcestershire Beacon; on this walk the highest point reached is on the 1,114 foot Herefordshire Beacon. With its strategic site, here was an extensive Iron Age fort. This is said to be one of the finest earthworks in England and dates from about the second century BC.

The final mile or so is a lovely track along the ridge then a winding path to the summit of the Beacon. It was near here that William Langland the great visionary, 'meatless and moneyless on Malvern Hill ... mused upon this dream' that became the *Vision of Piers Plowman*. We too can enjoy the spectacular views far across to the distant Welsh borderlands, before returning to our starting point.

THE WALK

1 At the far end of the car park walk along the vehicle way. This becomes a stony track to pass the reservoir, which supplies Malvern with water and was opened in 1895. A pathway then borders a brook through a wood. When the path divides keep descending to a bold track near a farm.

2 Turn right. The bridleway becomes a vehicle way and passes houses. Walk by a left-hand wood. When this ends

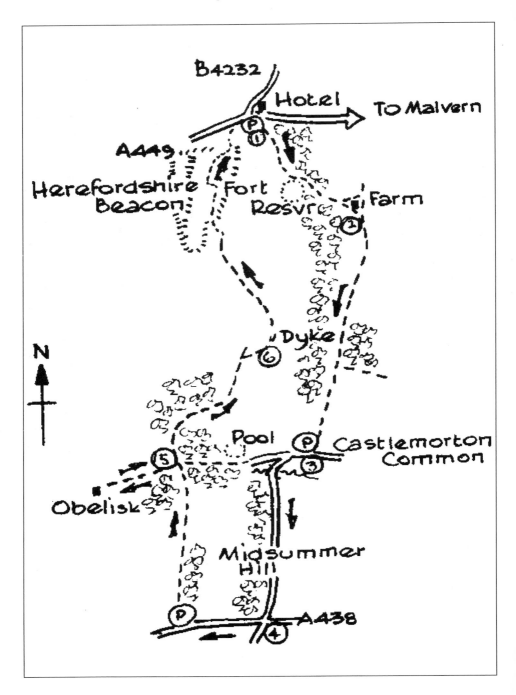

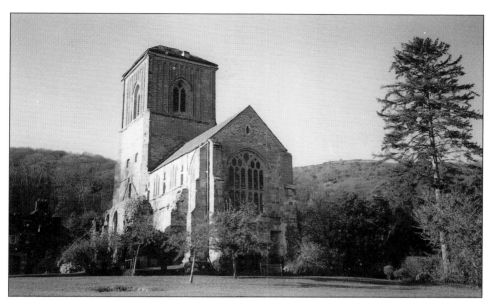

The delightful church at Little Malvern.

the vehicle way twists sharp left, but keep ahead along a path over Castlemorton Common to reach a lane.

3 Turn right. There is a junction of lanes. Bear left to cross a brook. (Note: For the shorter walk and to see the quarry pool keep on the lane ahead at the junction. The path goes through The Gullet woods to the gate to Eastnor Park. Rejoin the walk at point 5 below.) For the full walk follow the lane through the woods to the A438.

4 Turn right. within ½ mile and by a car park take a vehicle way on the right. The vehicle way becomes a wide stony track and leads to a meeting of tracks and the gate to Eastnor Park.

5 Turn left through the gate. Follow the path to the obelisk, then retrace your steps to the gate. Through this turn left. Follow the track through the woods. Out of the trees take a path right to climb to the ridge and the Dyke.

6 Swing left along the ridge. Follow the winding path to the top of the Herefordshire Beacon. From here paths and steps lead back to the car park.

PLACES of INTEREST

Near the car park is **Wynds Point** which was the home of Jenny Lind, the 'Swedish Nightingale'. As you drop down the hill through the woods you may glimpse the church at **Little Malvern**. This was once part of the Benedictine priory whose original charter was granted in 1125. After the walk music lovers may like to visit **Elgar's grave**. He is buried in the churchyard of the Catholic church at Little Malvern.

Walk 19
A PATHWAY UP BREDON HILL
Length : 5 miles

Sitting astride the King and Queen Rocks on Bredon Hill.

GETTING THERE: A mile westwards along the A44 from Evesham take the lane left signposted to Elmley Castle.

PARKING: There is a car park in the village along the Ashton under Hill road.

MAP: OS Landranger – Worcester and the Malverns 150 (GR 982411).

The round dome of Bredon Hill is like a huge whale quietly floating on a green sea. The upland is an outlier of the Cotswolds and therefore the countryside and villages are those fashioned by the limestone terrain. The fields which once were exclusively wide sheep runs are now stony and one admires the skill of the farmers who grow good crops on an inhospitable soil.

The chronicler William Cobbett when undertaking his *Rural Rides* wrote that from Bredon he could see 'one of the richest spots in England and I am fully convinced a richer spot is not to be seen in any country in the world'! Many composers and writers have

FOOD and DRINK

There are two inns in Elmley Castle. The Queen Elizabeth is rather unusual in that customers come primarily for the beer and the pub ambience rather than the food. Crisps are sold but you can unwrap your own sandwiches! (A separate restaruant serves meals Wednesday to Sunday). Telephone: 01386 710209. There is another pub, the Old Mill Inn serving such delicacies as moule mariniere and cashew nuts paella and rather exquisite pies. Telephone: 01386 710407.

found inspiration on the hill and we recall A. E. Housman writing of 'summertime on Bredon'.

The geology of the area has ensured that there is much variety of landscape on the walk. The upper layer of Bredon is composed of oolitic limestone but lower down are the lias clays; the delineation with the limestone cap is marked by a steep escarpment. The landslips have given the area a humpy appearance and rabbits love to live here. On the lower slopes the middle lias clays hold water but overlay impermeable clays. The resultant rather boggy regions created lush vegetation growth and springs for the old village settlements.

From Elmley Castle the walk rises to almost the 1,000 feet mark; a Mr Parsons from Kemerton decided to build a tower on the upland to take the height to this yardstick. The tower remains but now bristles with radio gadgets to ensure that low-flying aircraft go safely over the hill.

There are several other features on the summit. Near to the tower are the King and Queen Rocks – huge lumps of limestone around which much folklore and tales of fertility rites have been woven. Here too is a large Iron Age fort dating from the 2nd century BC. Within the fort area is the Banbury Stone where it is said Druid priests made human sacrifices.

Some of the slopes of Bredon are covered in woods with the beech trees especially beautiful. Through these trees herds of deer roam; they are rather elusive but may be spotted early in the morning.

Below the slopes is the chequered countryside of the Vale of Evesham. From the high land everything – the cottages and churches and tractors – looks out of Toytown. These are rich farmlands and the blossom in the orchards in late springtime is a delight. It is through this lovely countryside that

PLACES of INTEREST

The remains of **Elmley Castle** are only marked by the terraced slopes of a hill near to the present village. The site perhaps dates from Saxon times but the castle became important when it was extended by the Norman Beauchamps in 1086 and virtually replaced Worcester Castle. When the Beauchamps inherited Warwick Castle in 1269 the importance of Elmley Castle declined and the castle was in ruins by the early 16th century. There is still plenty to see in this pretty village where a brook runs alongside the main street. The inn is called the Queen Elizabeth and commemorates the visit by the monarch to Squire Savage in 1575; a rather fine inn sign depicts the scene. Nearby is the tree-clustered church which has many reminders of the Savages including a sundial on the front. At the other end of the street is the village cross where travellers have met since the 15th century.

The ancient village cross at Elmley Castle.

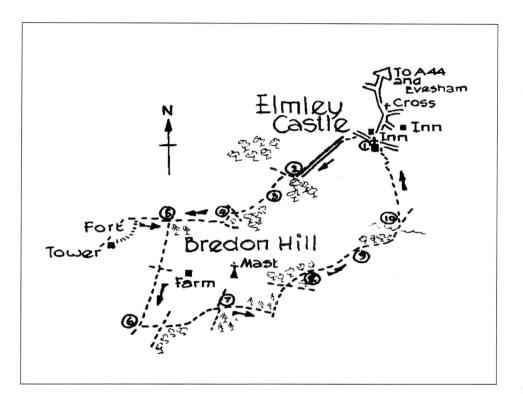

the walk brings you back to Elmley Castle.

THE WALK

1 Walk along the lane beside the Queen Elizabeth Inn. Within 300 yards take a signed path on the left. Cut over the field to rejoin the lane again. Turn left and follow the lane to the end.

2 The lane becomes a banked path. Go through a gate to a hill pasture. Swing left off the main track. Cross a cart track and climb the field, never far from a left-hand wire fence. In the far top left corner go through a gate.

3 Keep ahead. Soon the path becomes a stony cart track, still climbing. Pass a metal gate (do not go through) and stay on the cart track, still never far from the left-hand wire fence. In woods cross a banked track (near a 'Wild Flower' notice) and climb steeply to open rough pastureland.

4 Swing left (with woods now on your left) to climb to a corner gate. Do not go through but turn right (left-hand fence). Go through a gate by a fir wood.

5 Keep ahead to see the tower, fort and stones. Retrace your steps to the fir wood. Do not go through the gate but turn right to walk alongside the left-hand wall. Cross a stony farm track and maintain the heading through gates to a signed meeting of bridleways.

6   Turn left through a gate (a bridleway indicated by a blue arrow) and continue alongside a plantation of saplings on the right. At a tarmac farm road cross to the opposite tarmac farm road. A fir wood is reached. The tarmac way swings left to radio masts but keep ahead along a sandy farm way.

7   Keep ahead to pick up a line of fir trees on the left hand. At the end of the trees turn left to stay by the fir trees. Go through one gate and then another by woods. Take the signed bridleway into the woods almost opposite. The track drops steeply downhill.

8   Keep on the main track at a meeting of ways. Descend through bushes to a hunting gate. Keep descending over a rough pasture. Take care (a waymark post may be missing). Swing slightly right to keep descending (the path is less defined) down the V of the valley. (If you have missed the less-defined path and reach a gate into the castle site turn sharp right to regain the proper path.)

9   Go over the metal girder bridge and keep going downhill along a wide green path. When the way divides take the left-hand fork to cross a railway sleeper bridge. Turn left (a rather misleading waymark arrow may be here). Do not enter woods on the left but walk along a wide green path to pass through a blue gate.

10   Turn left over a footbridge and climb a stile to a pasture. Turn right. Walk the length of the field to a stile and footbridge in to an arable field. Turn left. Follow the path around the corner to the right to a stile on the left. Cross a meadow to another stile. Follow the path back to the church and Elmley Castle.

Walk 20
TO THE OLYMPICK GAMES ON DOVER'S HILL

Length : 4½ miles

Dover's Hill.

GETTING THERE: From the B4632 (Stratford-upon-Avon to Cheltenham road) take the B4081 at Mickleton to Chipping Campden.

PARKING: On the roadside near the church at Chipping Campden.

MAP: OS Landrandger – Stratford-upon-Avon and surrounding area 151 (GR 156395).

Chipping Campden is situated in the valley, but the hills above the town are magnificent viewpoints. Foremost is Dover's Hill, the site of ancient sports. It was in 1612 that Robert Dover, a London lawyer and an extrovert, started his 'games' on the breezy upland. There were such pastimes as shin-kicking, balancing on the hands and pitching the bar!

After several centuries of lively contest the 'Olympick Games' were ended in 1853 when rowdiness and riots got out of hand. The land was incensed that he raised money to purchase the hill and later it was presented to the National Trust for us to enjoy today. The Games were revived in 1951 and are held on the Friday evening following the Spring Bank Holiday, with a torchlight procession down the hill to the town at the conclusion of the sports.

The walk begins along Chipping Campden's mile-long main street, which was laid out as far back as the 12th century by Hugh de Gondeville, a favourite courtier of Henry II and Lord of the Manor. These were the burgage plots of the tradesmen with their houses fronting the street. Many fine houses were built in the 14th and 15th centuries for the merchants and

enclosed and the public excluded. Early in the 20th century there were plans to build a hotel on the spectacular site; Landseer Gibbs, an artist who fell in love with Chipping Campden, was so

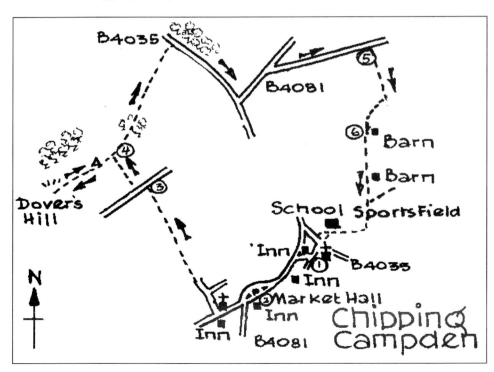

Almhouses at Chipping Campden.

woolstaplers who handled the wool and collected the taxes on behalf of the monarch. The great 'wool church' was rebuilt during this prosperous time.

Baptist Hicks was a London merchant who purchased the Manor in 1606 and was a great benefactor to the town. Near the entrance to the church is a gatehouse. This was the way into Campden House, a grand mansion built in a rather ornate oriental style by Hicks but ruined 30 years later during the Civil War.

The countryside outside the town is typical Cotswold landscape, with wide grassy areas where limestone-loving wild flowers flourish. Here a type of sheep (now almost extinct) called the Cotswold Lion once roamed; the sheep brought great prosperity to the area in the 14th and 15th centuries. Since the Second World War good husbandry has meant arable farming has taken over but this in turn has given the scenery more variety.

All around are skilfully constructed stone walls and you will even spot some recently rebuilt to demonstrate that old skill has not been lost. Buildings in the area are primarily of stone – honey-hued and weathered as though part of nature rather than man-made.

Below the hills, in the wide Vale of Evesham and the valley of the Avon, there are market gardens. On the walk you can see far across these lower lands to Bredon Hill, the Malverns and, nearer, the flat-topped Meon Hill with its ridges and hollows of the Iron Age fort (and tales of mysterious legends and folklore – there was even a murder on Valentine's Day in 1945!). On distant horizons are the Lickey, Clent and Clee Hills.

THE WALK

1 From the church walk along Church Street, passing Baptist Hicks' almshouses of 1612 on the right. On the left is a wheel dip, into which carts were trundled to soak the wooden wheels and prevent them from shrinking. The Eight Bells is the oldest inn in the town. It was built in the 15th century to house the workers who built the church. At the junction turn left along the High Street. On the right is William Grevel's House, and the Woolstaplers' Hall is on the left.

2 Pass the Market Hall (see the stone marking the official start of the Cotswold Way) and keep ahead at Sheep Street. By the Catholic church turn right. Keep ahead at junctions. The road becomes a vehicle way to a stile onto a footpath, which runs alongside a tractor way to a road.

3 Turn left, then right within 200 yards. The fenced path runs alongside a hedge to a stile into a meadow. At the marker post turn left to pass a triangulation plinth. Follow the meadow to the toposcope on Dover's Hill. Retrace your steps to the marker post and keep ahead.

4 Follow the waymarked bridleway (blue arrows) through sheep pastures and a wood. Drop down to a bridlegate onto a road. Turn right. At a junction by an old toll house turn left. Within 300 yards veer right along a narrow lane (signed Hidcote).

PLACES of INTEREST

At the bottom end of the High Street in Chipping Campden is Sheep Street. A few yards along is the old **Silk Mill**. Built in 1790 it made ribbons but was redundant after 60 years. In 1902 the place was the centre for the Guild of Handicrafts. The Guild, led by the visionary C.R. Ashbee, came from the East End of London and attempted to counter mass-produced goods by making hand-crafted items. Sadly, it failed within six years. Some craftsmen stayed and their descendants still work in the old mill. Visit the little museum there. Telephone: 01386 841417 for details of opening times.

5 After ¼ mile take a signed path through a gate on the right. In the field walk alongside a left-hand border. In a corner go through a hedge gap and turn right. Keep at the edge of the field then turn a corner to walk up the slope.

6 Pass a barn, then climb the stiles by farm buildings. Maintain the heading to join a meeting of paths. Still keep ahead, now walking alongside a sports field on the right. Follow the path around to the right to still stay by the school grounds. Follow the arrowed way to reach a road by the church back at the starting place in Chipping Campden.